ARISE...Intercessors Arise!

A Manual For the Birthing, Calling, Training and Restoration of Prayer Warriors

MARIA L. HARBAJAN

Foreword by Esther Ilnisky

outskirtspress

DENVER, COLORADO

ARISE...Intercessors Arise!
A Manual for the Birthing, Calling, Training and Restoration of Prayer Warriors
All Rights Reserved.
Copyright © 2015 Maria L. Harbajan
v3.0

Scripture Quotations from:
- ASV – American Standard Version, 1901, published by Thomas Nelson & Sons.
- KJV – King James Version, 1769
- NAS – New American Standard Bible - "Scripture taken from the NEW AMERICAN STANDARD BIBLE®, Copyright © 1960,1962,1963,1968,1971,1972,1973,1975,1977,1995 by The Lockman Foundation. Used by permission." (www.Lockman.org)
- NKJV – New King James Version - Scripture taken from the New King James Version®. Copyright © 1982 by Thomas Nelson. Used by permission. All rights reserved.
- The Message – "Scripture taken from The Message. Copyright © 1993, 1994, 1995, 1996, 2000, 2001, 2002. Used by permission of NavPress Publishing Group."

Cover Photo © 2015 thinkstockphotos.com All rights reserved - used with permission.

Outskirts Press, Inc.
http://www.outskirtspress.com

ISBN: 978-1-4787-4867-0

Outskirts Press and the "OP" logo are trademarks belonging to Outskirts Press, Inc.

PRINTED IN THE UNITED STATES OF AMERICA

Affectionately dedicated to my beloved husband and friend, Devon S. Harbajan, my constant encourager; the one who lovingly supports me through thick and thin; the motivator behind the writing of this book. One who exemplifies Christ within and outside of his home.

In memory of our older son, Qowayne, who is presently with the Lord but in his few years in life taught us how much our hearts could love a child who was not from our own loins.

To DeMario, our beloved son, who loves Jesus. A young worshipper, intercessor, lover of the Word of God. Our special "gift from God"!

This book is also dedicated to all the Generals of Intercession and other intercessors who have faithfully stood with me in ministry through the years, when I abounded and when I abased; and to every member of the Body of Christ who dared to stand in-the-gap for God. My heart swells with thanksgiving for all of you.

Contents

Acknowledgements

I wish to express my deepest appreciation to my husband, Devon, who believed in me and encouraged my talent in writing.

To my accountability partner, Sharon Nash, who has always watched my back since High School and did so through the writing of this book.

To Judith Taylor who willingly volunteered her help in editing, proofreading and formatting this book.

To my mother, a constant fan; a prayer support for decades.

To all my mentors, Bishop Peter Morgan, Newton Gabbidon, Esther Ilnisky, Carroldean Moore, for modelling a consistent intercessory life.

To all my pastors, elders, disciplers and teachers who built block-upon-block in my life over the years to produce this building for God.

To Shirley-Ann Chong and remembering the late Rev. Vivie White who stood boldly and supported me in ministry at a time when I truly needed my hands strengthened. Their "fuelling" through prayer and encouragement went a far way to rejuvenate my vision.

To all the NIPNOJ Family, especially the Intercessors Mobilization Campers and young Boot Campers, Friends and Family Members. Thanks for dreaming with me; praying with me and staying with me. Your support has been invaluable.

Foreword

Maria was Divinely destined from the foundations of the earth to carry the Intercessory Prayer Mantle...and she has carried it well.

This book should be required reading for every serious, committed intercessor. In it, Maria is candid, honest and plainspoken of herself. She offers volumes of revelations and truths for anyone who takes seriously the *ministry* of intercession. Whether you are a beginner or a seasoned intercessor, you will learn, as I have, from this excellent work.

My first encounter with Maria occurred on a Jamaican mountaintop. She refers to it in her opening chapter. However, I didn't have a clue about her state of mind – or state of being - as she describes her 'then' self. I saw a young lady, an avid intercessor. I didn't know that she began experiencing the journey of the Mantle at the ripe old age of fifteen! She really amazed me.

Oh yes, of course the enemy would, through the years, devise plots to "overthrow" her (her own words). Although I was among those who walked with her through some deep, murky waters of life, her own *DETERMINATION, DRIVE, DEDICATION and SPIRITUAL STAMINA* – kept her afloat – and then some.

Just look where God has her now! She's known worldwide. She continues to wear the Mantle worthily.

[Esther Ilnisky, founder, Esther Network International and Children's Global Prayer Movement]

Preface

Many books have been written on intercession and many have shaped my own life. Prayer generals like Cindy Jacobs, Esther Ilnisky, Tom Hess and Peter Wagner have done great jobs in writing to guide intercessors. There was however a constant cry that kept coming at me from two camps: First and foremost, the Camp of Pastors and shepherds of intercessors who were at their wits end with the intercessors in their fellowships who they found difficult to understand and lead. In some instances, pastors confessed that they shut down the intercessory ministry out of a real or imagined fear that it would do more harm than good for the Church.

The second camp of the concerned was the intercessors themselves who felt misunderstood by their leaders and at the extreme end of multiple reactions, ostracized. Having listened to and counselled with both sides, the Holy Spirit spoke to me over time about teaching intercessors how to be balanced in this ministry. Hence the birth of a course on Intercession and related fields geared towards equipping and certifying intercessors to serve correctly within their own local Churches and in the Marketplaces. The challenge then was to produce a text which would adequately address the aforementioned concerns while accomplishing the desired end results.

This manual is a text that every pastor who believes in the role of intercessors and the necessity of this ministry for the support of their own ministry, should read carefully. This guidepost is for every practicing intercessor, even those who have fallen by the wayside, to read for the rejuvenation of their spirit-man and the restoration of their call; to bring them to new heights and depths in intercession. It is written for any believer who is convicted that prayer is specifically needed to fulfil the mandate of the Kingdom of God and therefore points to the need for the entire Body of Christ to intercede.

This book is divinely inspired to give a fatal blow to the lies of the kingdom of darkness whose cohorts have diabolically engineered dysfunctional relationships between leaders and intercessors in order to destroy the prayer engine in the Church. Well, the devil is a liar! He cannot and will never stop God's praying people. My prayer is that God will restore within these affected Churches and among His faithful intercessors, all the benefits of intercession and more.

May all who read this book, including the unbeliever, come to a deep knowledge of Christ and find themselves in an intimate relationship with the Godhead, always running to God in prayer; no longer wanting to be missing during corporate times of prayer; and having an unquenchable appetite for the constant presence of God in their lives. Be blessed.

CHAPTER 1

No One Taught Me How to Pray

Prayer is essentially the expression of our heart longing for love. It is not so much the listing of our requests but the breathing of our own deepest request, to be united with God as fully as possible.

Eugene Peterson

NO ONE TAUGHT me how to pray, at least not initially. Mine was the honour, after only being saved for a few hours at fifteen years old, to find myself kneeling at my bedside, saying prayers of thanksgiving, repentance and supplication. No one spoke to me about going home and confessing all my sins, turning away and changing my mind about the way I used to live and instantly asking God to take away my wicked ways and immoral practices. I can only conclude that it was the power of the Holy Spirit that drove me to simply "talk to God" which is a simple way of defining prayer.

The Holy Spirit continued to lead me into the presence of God, just to talk with Him. So for the years that followed, like a student who immediately wanted to do her homework before anything else, I religiously, upon arriving home, went into my room, locked the door behind me and began to pray. Praying for my friends, praying for my teachers and family to become Christians; praying for an assurance of salvation when I sinned. Whatever ailed me, I would pray. Whatever was the burden of the day, would find itself leaking out of my soul into only one person's ears, my Father's, in the form of a prayer.

It was a good thing that I found a friend in Jesus in those early years. Not sure, if it was that I reminded my Christian school-mates of Saul before he became Paul, but for one whole year, my fifth form year, the Christians, though some of them knew about my change of life, gave me a wide circle and observed me from afar. It was as if there was a disbelief that my life could be so radically turned around. It was a lonely first year with Christ with the exception of the Holy Spirit who drew me into a prayer closet daily to pour out my heart in prayer; and for a group that I had joined who met in the Chapel Gardens at the University of the West Indies (UWI). Again, most of them were older than I was. They were mainly tertiary students.

It was as a young adult that I began to hear the word Intercession. I had joined a group of committed Christians who gathered weekly for prayer at my Church. Still, it remained only a word, until an intercessors' retreat was being called for the group. Being one of the youngest members of the group and not wanting to be out of order if I did not turn up, I mustered enough courage to ask if I was expected to attend. "Of course," was the leader's response. "You are an intercessor." I am? I thought to myself and mulled it over in my mind. I needed to find out exactly who was an intercessor and what were the requirements of this role. Little did I know that that was the beginning of a lifetime of learning and living and reproducing in this role.

Who Is an Intercessor?

The best way to define Intercession is to explain what PRAYER is. Prayer is conversing with God - expressing a need or desire, beseeching, entreating, vowing. *(Vine's Expository Dictionary of Biblical Words).* It is usually subjective, meditative and conversational, with personal requests or for immediate concerns. The best definition I have heard of prayer came from a child who boldly put up his hand in a seminar to answer my question: What is prayer? "Prayer is a friend spending time talking with another friend and that is God," was his response. As simple as it sounded, it bowled me for a while. Mmm. I suddenly realized that this was what I was doing from my childhood, talking everyday with my Friend! I believe that if more of us adopted this view of prayer, we would hasten more to the place of prayer.

There are however, different TYPES OF PRAYERS: Petition, supplication, thanksgiving, intercession and vowing. Some would add, the Prayer of Repentance, the Prayer of Faith, the Prayer of Agreement and the Prayer of Binding and Loosing. The type of prayer chosen depends on the particular request or expression to God that one would want to offer. There are also public prayers and private prayers; again, the distinctive expressions are subject to the context of the prayer.

What is INTERCESSION? It is the act of going 'in between' or 'on behalf' of someone else. To plead, petition on behalf of another in trouble or difficulty; to intervene, intercept, mediate (Webster's Dictionary). The Bible, in principle, defines intercession as "standing in-the-gap" or to "step in the breach" (Ezek. 22:30). One of my mentors, Esther Ilnisky of Esther Network International in her own definition of intercession usually points out that it has mostly to do with matters of ETERNAL significance, dealing with the spirit world in offensive authoritative warfare.

The best way to illustrate intercession is using a picture that we are very familiar with. It is the picture of a lawyer. A lawyer becomes familiar with a case and with the knowledge he has, stands before the judge to appeal for mercy. His aim is usually to prove innocence on behalf of an accused party or if the party is guilty, to plead for mercy or leniency. The "accused" often says very little while the lawyer does most of the talking on his behalf. Sounds a lot like Moses and the prophets in Israel. He was always praying for the people and the nation. This is what intercession is about. It involves praying for others, whether it is the church, the government, the community, the workplace or speaking to God on behalf of a person in need. (Ephesians 1:15-18; Coloss.1: 9-11)

BIBLICAL EXAMPLES

ABRAHAM

Genesis 18:16 – 19:29 gives us the account of Abraham and the destruction of Sodom. In 18:17, God asks Himself a question: "And the Lord said, Shall I hide from Abraham the thing which I do?"(KJV) Abraham's relationship with God made Him want to take Abraham into His own council. God was about to destroy the city because the "cry was great" and their sin was grievous (v. 20). The heart of the intercessor is stirred up in Abraham as soon as God reveals His will to him. "… but Abraham stood yet before the Lord. And Abraham drew near, and said, Will you destroy the righteous with the wicked?" (v. 22 - KJV), The mediation, transaction, negotiation now begins – the role that oftentimes one has to play as an intercessor. Abraham begins by asking God, "Suppose you find 50 righteous?" and counts down, "'45'... '40' ... '30' ... '20' ... '10'?" (vs 24 – 28 - KJV).

The account proves that intercession works. The Bible records in Gen. 19:29, that "God remembered Abraham and sent Lot out of the midst of the overthrow." Not only Lot, but the rest of his family who were righteous!

DANIEL

Daniel chapter 9 describes a man of God who was truly an intercessor. He studied the Word of God and sought to understand God's will through such meditation. " …. I understood by books." (v. 2 - KJV). This would have been, for example, the book of Jeremiah. This understanding of God's Word flowed naturally into some other important disciplines of an intercessor – prayer, fasting and repentance. "And I set my face unto the Lord to seek by prayer and supplications with fasting, sackcloth and ashes." (v. 3 - KJV).

Daniel, as an intercessor, models for us some important prerequisites: The conviction of an intercessor leading to no compromises, especially when it comes to God's glory (2:30); The stance of an intercessor that one cannot afford the deadly cost of jeopardizing one's role by defilement of the body (1:8); A death to self that will enable one to "stand" and to continue PRAYING even when threatened with physical death (6:10); A standing in- the- gap to facilitate the deliverance of a nation that might be under a curse manifested in desolation (9:2,11); A critical identification with the sins of a people – Identificational Intercession – which qualifies the intercessor to stand before God to represent his/her people (9:5 - 19). It is interesting that God usually seeks for a "man among them" to stand in-the-gap (Ezek. 22:30). Then there was in Daniel, the invaluable attitude of submission and dependency on the Ultimate Judge, for mercy (9:4,9,16) knowing that this mercy can come as a result of the intercessor first dealing with the sins of his nation (9:5-14), thus clearing the way for atonement.

Why Is an Intercessor So Important?

If Israel could not do without an intercessor, can we? I can think of many personal benefits that intercession brings to an individual – a life that is removed from self-centredness to caring for and serving others through prayer; a continuous growth in the dynamics of prayer which includes an endless flow of answers to prayer, even if one has to wait for a while for these answers; a constant feeling of being led beside "still waters" which restores the soul, even while praying for others; watching your own needs being met, while standing in-the-gap for others. These are only some of the benefits on a personal level. But why is it so important for a family, a community, the workplace, a Church and a nation to have intercessors? What is it that intercession does that other types of praying might not do?

Intercession can **avert God's wrath** upon your family, community, nation. We have the Scriptural example of Moses standing in-the-gap for Israel when they sinned in the account of the worship of the Golden Calf (Exodus 32:9 – 14). What is critical to note about Moses as another great example of an intercessor is that he represented the people. He refused the "singular" blessing that he could have received and instead, continued pleading with God on behalf of the sinful nation of Israel. Can you imagine, Moses receiving, as it were, a "blank cheque" from God and giving it back – ignoring it completely? (Exod. 32:10). What would you and I have done?

Moses brought some strong arguments to God and God listened. He brought reference to God's character and reputation, even citing how the heathen nation, from which He just delivered His people would view Him if He carried out His threat (vs 11, 12). He then appealed to another aspect of God – His covenant-keeping nature – that He does not break His promises (v 13). What could move God more than a man "among them" standing up and declaring I know WHO you are and who these people are to You? God listened and acted. Verse 14 tells us: "Then the Lord relented and did not bring on His people the disaster He threatened." (KJV)

There was also another occasion when God relented when Israel, as a nation, sinned against Him. Numbers 14:1-20 gives us this account of Israel grumbling about going into the Promise Land. Obviously, this truly provoked God's wrath. Moses brought similar challenges to God and the results were the same. Verse 20 records God as saying, "I have pardoned according to your word." (Updated KJV) What power a man or woman of God can have with God, just by standing in-the-gap before Him on behalf of others.

We do have another account however, which brings out another result. What is it that could have made the difference? Ezek. 22:18-29 outlines for us the state of Israel – corruption at all levels and in every sphere. A nation truly in degradation. God goes searching for the one thing that would make a difference to Him in the midst of that crisis so that He would not have to destroy that nation. "And I sought for a man among them, that should make up the hedge, and stand in the gap before me for the land, that I should not destroy it: but I found none." (Ezek. 22:30 - KJV). It is clear that there was a problem - God could not find ONE person that could stand up for the nation, perhaps in a similar way that Moses and Abraham did. The consequences of this fact were painful and is an encouragement to every intercessor to press on in that role, in spite of the opposition and other trials that he or she might be facing. This is what came upon Israel:

"Therefore have I poured out mine indignation upon them; I have consumed them with the fire of my wrath: their own way have I recompensed upon their heads, saith the Lord GOD." (Eze 22:31 - KJV).

MODERN DAY EXAMPLES

There are countless examples of prayers of intercession averting catastrophe in my own nation, Jamaica, when it was clear that we had, by our corruption, stirred up God's wrath and His hand was moving against us. We have had numerous hurricanes, heading for us as categories 1 and 2, and the intercessors have stood in-the-gap repenting, appealing to God on behalf of the nation, while the national and international weather reports were showing those hurricanes heading straight for the island. We knew we would not have any chance of survival as the strength of those winds and the amount of rain that would be dumped on us would have wiped out our infrastructure, not to mention the loss of lives!

Something mysterious usually happens which we can only interpret as the mercy of God – a miracle! Those hurricanes would weaken to a lesser category; make an unexplained turn away from the island; or behave erratically and disintegrate before reaching the island. While the nation braced for the worse, we saw the sure Hand of divine mercy. All glory goes to Him for those underserved mercies.

A second reason why Intercession is important has to do with the Lord's own teaching. **Jesus taught us to do so in the "Lord's Prayer"**. In Matthew 6:10, we were taught by Jesus Himself to pray: "Your Kingdom come, Your will be done on earth." (NASB) This we could deem as having a Global Perspective in prayer. This is not about my personal needs or just praying out of what I want or like for myself or others. This is a pointed principle in praying that focuses us on what God wants for His world, which includes our families, communities, Churches, workplaces and the nations. It is interesting to note that this aspect of prayer even preceded prayers for daily bread, deliverance from evil, etc. Does that speak to us about what God sees as priority?

Matthew 11:12 could assist in giving clarification regarding this principle. "And from the days of John the Baptist until now the kingdom of heaven suffers violence, and the violent take it by force." (NKJV) Michael Pedrin (http://clearbibleanswers.org) offers an interpretation of this verse that I believe is a plausible explanation of what Jesus meant. Pedrin wrote:

> "There is a war that rages behind the scene. It is a spiritual war. Only the ones who "press" forward can be victorious. Every kind of war is violent, and there is no exception to this War of wars. Unless we are "violent"- having holy zeal and deter-mination-we will never win it. We have got to strive and press forward every inch in this spiritual battle. If we are hoping to be victorious doing nothing about it, we will be devoured by the roaring lion…We strive and wrestle it out not physically with our fellow humans, but spiritually with the powers of darkness."

The Apostle Paul was quick to remind us that we are not wrestling in the flesh, but we do wrestle. Our war is against unseen forces called principalities, powers, the rulers of the darkness of this world and spiritual wickedness in high places. (Ephesians 6:12)

How much do we love God? Do we love Him enough to put aside our personal preferences in how we pray and to take on this warfare to ensure that everything that our Master, Friend and King desires, comes to pass? How we defend the Kingdom of God is one of the acid tests of how much we are devoted to the ruler of this Kingdom.

Thirdly, Intercession is important because before and after all is tried in the natural, **it can avert the plans of wicked people and governments**. The Book of Esther paints this truth vividly. The king Artaxerxes, who reigned from India to Ethiopia, over a hundred provinces, had an unwise counsellor and leader in his Legislative council. Haman had an evil heart and was hateful towards Mordecai, a man of God, and an intercessor. He therefore convinced the king to kill all the Jews, knowing that this was Mordecai's race.

The Edict went out – "Kill all the Jews." (Esther 4:7, 8). The intercessor in Mordecai rose up in faith and strength and he went before the king's gate, risking his life (Esther 4:1-3). Other Jews joined in fasting and intercession within their own provinces. When Mordecai challenged his relative Queen Esther to step in-the-gap on behalf of her people and she responded with fear and reluctance, his response was twofold: to state what God could do to deliver his people and what could befall those who failed to intercede.

Mordecai responded with a WARNING which could be applied in our lives today: Failure to intercede might mean ill upon your family, community, church and nation.

> *"Then Mordecai commanded to answer Esther, Think not with thyself that thou shalt escape in the king's house, more than all the Jews. For if thou altogether hold thy peace at this time, then shall there enlargement and deliverance arise to the Jews from another place; but thou and thy father's house shall be destroyed: and who knows whether thou art come to the kingdom for such a time as this?"*
>
> *(Esther 4:13, 14- KJV)*

Esther's obedience to intercede brought victory to her people and the wicked leader, Haman, was destroyed as his own plots against the people of God backfired (Esther 6:4, 10-12; 7:7-10)!

Another reason why intercession is a must for us now is that **this is what Jesus is doing full-time now** - so we are joining Him – praying with Him what is on His heart. Hebrews 7:25 tells us that, "He always lives to make intercession for them." (NKJV) We could call Jesus the Everlasting Intercessor since His priesthood and stance of standing in-the-gap never ends!

In Clarke's Commentary on the Bible, the commentary on this verse indicates that "The phrase εντυγχανειν τινι, to make intercession for a person, has considerable latitude of meaning. It signifies,

i. To come to or meet a person on any cause whatever.

ii. To intercede, pray for, or entreat in the behalf of another.

iii. To defend or vindicate a person.

iv. To commend.

v. To furnish any kind of assistance or help.

vi. And, with the preposition κατα, against, to accuse, or act against another in a judicial way.

(Clarke's Commentary on the Bible)

It is amazing to see God at work in All-night Prayer Meetings for the three decades I have participated in them. Whether in the USA or in Jamaica, the Spirit of God is alive and vibrant in many of those meetings throughout the night. The thought usually occurs to me that Jesus takes no rest and therefore He is up with us all night. Another way to put it is that we are joining Him all night in what He is doing all the time. Out of this notion, the All-night meetings were dubbed, 'One Night With the King'.

What is even more amazing is to see the children, from as young as five years old, in our All-night meetings, not sleeping on a pillow on the Church bench or snuggled under a comforter sleeping the night away, but up all night until daylight, praying in creative ways with the use of prayer tools. They too are praying for nations, families and their friends. It is Jesus Who energizes the children to join Him in intercession in the wee hours of the morning!

If there is one reason why intercession is important and a reason never to be ignored is that there are **consequences for not interceding.** Ezekiel 8 paints the disturbing picture of Israel in their apostasy and idolatry. Even the spiritual leaders had gone astray. It is what God did however, prior to judging that is of interest to us at this point. In chapter 9, God placed a mark upon and spared those who were interceding and had a heart that was disturbed by the abominations but punished those who did not. This is a Selah moment as we ponder these things.

> *"And the LORD said unto him, Go through the midst of the city, through the midst of Jerusalem, and set a mark upon the foreheads of the men that sigh and that cry for all the abominations that be done in the midst thereof. And to the others he said in my hearing, Go ye after him through the city, and smite: let not your eye spare, neither have ye pity: …but come not near any man upon whom is the mark; and begin at my sanctuary. Then they began with the elders which were before the house."*

> *(Ezekiel 9:4 – 6 - KJV)*

A final general reason why it is important to intercede is that **we could be sinning if we don't.** Samuel, the priest, prophet and judge in Israel understood his role as a leader. He knew that it was important to stand in-the-gap when Israel sinned. "Far be it from me," he said, "that I should sin against the Lord in ceasing to pray for you." (1 Samuel 12:23 - NKJV).

I have often wondered how many times we could have saved lives, averted danger, changed some events, if we obediently responded to the voice of the Lord, sometimes when He awakens us before we are ready, and prompts us to pray. There are so many testimonies of persons who were delivered out of the hands of criminals and when they shared their account, there was someone who was disturbed in their spirit enough to pray for them, not knowing what was occurring and could have befallen them at that moment. Can you imagine how grateful those recipients of prayer must have felt. Would we have been grateful too? If so, we should be willing to be the active intercessor that God can use to save lives.

CHAPTER 2

Growth in Prayer Requires Knowledge
of the Principles in the Practice of Prayer

There is no way to learn to pray except by praying. No reasoned philosophy by itself ever taught a soul to pray. But to the man who fulfills the conditions, the problems are met in the indisputable fact of answered prayer and the joy of conscious fellowship with God.

Anonymous

MANY HAVE WONDERED why the disciples asked Jesus to teach them to pray. Did they not have knowledge of prayer before? Weren't they practicing to pray even from their youth in the synagogues? What could have prompted this request? There must have been something in the way that Jesus prayed that expressed a depth in praying; a height that He reached while praying; a result that He got through praying and possibly a way that He was as He prepared Himself to speak, on some occasions, all night with His Father. It was possibly something that was beyond the ordinary and stimulated a desire in them to have the same connection with their Father.

How Should We Prepare for Intercession?

CLEANSING

One of the worst experiences is to know that you are speaking to someone about something that is important and he is not listening – not paying attention to you at all. This might spark feelings of frustration, rejection and some might feel insulted. One of the first principles in preparation for prayer is to avoid this. In Psalm 66:18, we are instructed, "If I regard iniquity in my heart the Lord will not hear me." (KJV) What is iniquity? It is immorality, evil, injustice, mischief, idolatry, vanity, sin. There is something about the nature of God that cannot stand up in the face of sin. Hence, His turning away from His Son when the sins of the world were dumped on Him on the cross. "Jesus cried with a loud voice, saying, Eloi, Eloi, lama sabachthani?" Which, when translated means, "My God, my God, why hast thou forsaken me?" (Mar 15:34 - KJV)

When we love someone and learn what repels them, we do not make it our practice to do that very thing. We do and should try to avoid it. Out of our love for God, we should avoid doing the things, as laid out in the Scriptures that repel Him. Since prayer is talking to God and ensuring that He listens to us so that He will choose to respond to our prayers, we need to, from the beginning of this discourse, ask Him to cleanse us from all of our sins. We can never be worthy by ourselves to stand in-the-gap for anyone but applying the cleansing blood of Jesus gives us that status before God (Heb. 4:15, 16).

Jesus was able to make a proclamation in John 14:30 which is one that we should be aspiring to make.

"...for the prince of this world cometh, and hath nothing in me."

(KJV)

Jesus made one thing clear. The prince of this world, Satan himself, is going to show up on the doorsteps of our lives. This is not a maybe and has nothing to do with how righteous we are. But one thing is sure. When he shows up, he should have NO claim on us - He should have nothing in common with us; there should be nothing in us that belongs to Him and he should have no power over us. Jesus exemplified this in His ministry.

MEDITATING ON HIS WORD

The Psalmist David is oftentimes identified primarily with worship. However, there is another aspect of him that is admirable and that made him powerful. Our clue is in Psalm 119:97: "Oh, how love I your law! It is my meditation all the day." (KJV) It sounds as if he is speaking about God's Word the way persons speak of their love of favourite foods, hobbies, television programmes.

The Word has to get inside of us first before we can meditate on it. Intercessors must develop the discipline of studying God's Word which is a prerequisite for praying intelligently. This is the primary way to know the will of God so that we can know how to pray for God's Kingdom to come and His will to be done (Matt. 6:10). In the three decades that I have been learning about intercession, the mistake has been made by me and by others, of praying opinions and desires on behalf of others, including God. A careful study of God's Word would have afforded us the knowledge of what He desires for the individual or situation. The Word of God does help to bring objectivity in prayer.

Joshua was another man of God that we associate more with what he did, which was to courageously rage wars on behalf of Israel. We sometimes forget that he too was a man of the Word. In Josh. 1:8, God challenged him never to make "this book of the law" depart from him but to meditate on it day and night. Did he follow through on this? There is no indication in Scriptures that he did not.

WAITING ON THE LORD

Apart from disappointment in unanswered prayers, perhaps the next hardest experience in the prayer lives of many is waiting on God. This has been since time immemorial, as we have heard numerous accounts of the patriarchs who have done many senseless acts, based on the anxiety that often comes from feeling that delay might be denial; and what it will cost, if we are denied by the only divine Helper that we have. Yet, waiting has produced the opposite and positive effect that impatience and fear did not. The difference is clear in the classic account of Ishmael and Isaac (Genesis 16, 17, 21), which many believe was a conflict produced by an inability to wait on God's timing and has had its consequences outlived even in modern times in the impasse between the Jews and the Arabs.

A positive account of "waiting on God" comes from King Jehoshaphat in II Chronicles 18. It is noteworthy to point out that this king, before going into battle, turned to prayer. 11 Chron. 18:4: "And Jehoshaphat said to the king of Israel, inquire first, I pray you, for the Word of the Lord today." (KJV) 20:3 - "And Jehoshaphat feared, and set himself to seek the LORD, and proclaimed a fast throughout all Judah." (KJV)

His responses that followed this enquiring display a Godly posture, one which each intercessor should have in praying. (i) We do not know what to do but our eyes are upon you (v. 12); (ii) and as they went forth, Jehoshaphat stood and said, Hear me, O Judah, and you inhabitants of Jerusalem; Believe in the LORD your God, so shall you be established; believe his prophets, so shall you prosper (2Ch 20:20). The victory that they encountered was a glorious result of waiting on and trusting God in their circumstances (20:17 – 30). (KJV)

An apt analogy of waiting can be found in the picture of a waiter in a restaurant who patiently stands aside anticipating the call of the persons being served and keeping that posture, as long as it takes, until the patrons are fully served. In some cases this takes hours of standing, walking back and forth, having to deal with sometimes unpleasant and displeasing customers but not moving out of his position of being a waiter.

PRAISE AND WORSHIP

A great secret that warriors in the Old and New Testament learnt was the place of Praise and Worship in prayer and spiritual warfare. Praise and Worship are good faith-builders and Satan and his hosts hate it. God even speaks of how powerful it is in the lives of children because out of their mouths He has ordained praise for a reason – "because of your enemies, that you might silence the enemy and avenger." (Psalm 8:2 - NKJV).

Psalm 149 is another classic Psalm. Verses 6-9 speaks about the high praises of God being in the mouths of the saints (praise and worship); a two-edged sword in their hand (Word of God), again it is to execute vengeance upon all God's enemies!

In 1 Sam. 16:15 – 23, David, through his worshipful playing of an instrument, brought relief and deliverance to King Saul, and Jehoshaphat, through his recognition of the place and power of praise in warfare, witnessed how praise brought confusion in the camp of the enemy (2 Chron. 20:21 – 23).

FORGIVENESS

A major blockage to prayer is unforgiveness, therefore a door-opener to an intercessor getting his prayer through to divine ears, is **forgiveness**. This has to do with releasing from our hearts, anyone who might have offended us in any way. A difficult topic; a difficult task and for many, a difficult process. Yet it must be done. God commands us to forgive and in the same measure that He has forgiven us of all of our sins (Luke 11:4)!

WHAT FORGIVENESS IS NOT

Forgiveness is **not** an emotional decision. If it were, we would have to wait on our emotions to be healed before we could even consider forgiving. It is **not** a fleshly – motivated decision but one that comes through divine persuasion. God does give us the grace, whether we are Christians or not, to forgive. It is **not** the condoning of another person's wrong done to us or to another.

It is simply saying, I am making a rational decision and a deliberate attempt not to keep recalling the sin of another. I am being divinely motivated to honestly release this individual from my heart now with a willingness to sincerely BLESS the offender and to **wish him well**! Think about it. Isn't forgiveness one of the greatest weapons against Satan – the accuser of the brethren before God (Rev. 12:10-11)? Isn't it the greatest weapon to destroy his mission to our hearts and lives, to steal, kill and destroy (John 10:10)? How many times have we had to forgive and realize that we too have caused offence to another?

Some External Ways for an Intercessor to Prepare

The intercessor's prayer life is different from the ordinary Christian's. He, being called to intercede for others will need to have props for prayer. Some of these include prayer agendas – a list of items to pray about daily, weekly, monthly. This prayer agenda could be divided into items of Prayer for the Church, the Community, the Nation, Other Nations, the Workplace, Ministry, Friends and Family. *Newspaper clippings* can be used to intercede over news items. In some instances, it is good to have a *prayer partner / partners* that you can access, since one chases a thousand but two can put ten thousand to flight (Deut. 32:30; Ecclesiastes 4:9 – 12).

CHAPTER 3

Intercession...a Call for All or a Ministry

God shapes the world by prayer. The more praying there is in the world the better the world will be, the mightier the forces against evil...

E.M.Bounds

IN SOME PEOPLE'S minds, the work of intercession is for a few chosen and usually elderly persons who have weathered certain storms; won many battles with the Enemy; and not have too many items left on their plates in life and so can now give themselves to intercession. With this picture in mind, and in some instances, what is the reality in many churches, persons have not thought about the necessity of interceding, except in a general call in the Church service to pray for a common threat. Intercession however, comes naturally when one is close to God's heart. How can we be close to someone and yet not be affected by the things that breaks that person's heart?

A Call for All to Intercede

In Ezekiel chapter 9, there was one description of the persons who God spared. It was those who "sigh and that cry for all the abominations" that were done (Ezekiel 9:4). There is one underlying factor that He is looking for - the ones who are truly **'touched' by the things that touch His heart** and would take any necessary steps to **do something about it**, by their constant intercessions, supplications, speaking out, repenting and bringing forth fruit of repentance (II Chron. 7:14)!

The truth is, when judgment comes, every sector of the society gets touched – all age groups, the Church and secular society (Ezekiel 9:6). The children; He begins with the household of faith and first with the leaders (I Peter 4:17); He is not afraid to 'defile' the place of worship that is no longer serving its purpose (v. 7) BUT He is very careful to preserve those who look like Him; smell like Him; have the **"mark of His suffering"** on their foreheads (Rev. 7:3; 9:4)! We have seen in Scriptures that such a mark, God's mark, will not automatically come upon those who had great ministries in the Kingdom of God but upon those who truly were so connected to His heart that, like Jesus, they could only do what they saw their Father doing.

It usually is when the "cup overflows in God's sight" and there is no turning back on His part, that He judges. This is why it is necessary for all God's people to stand in-the-gap now when there is a wind of grace (II Chronicles 7:13-15)! God calls for "My people" which includes ALL the people who belong to Him to intercede and come before Him in true repentance, if He has to visit the land with disaster of any kind.

Intercession as a Ministry

THE CALL AS WATCHMAN

"I have set watchmen upon thy walls, O Jerusalem, which shall never hold their peace day nor night: ye that make mention of the LORD, keep not silence, And give him no

rest, till he establish, and till he make Jerusalem a praise in the earth."

(Isaiah 62:6 – 7 - KJV)

God is the One who chooses and "sets up" watchmen upon the "walls" of Churches, communities and nations. This is not a self-appointed position. The word **watchman** refers to a "military watchman or guard", for example a "keep" on a castle. It is a security guard.

God, Himself, sets up a particular type of people who "shall never hold their peace day nor night". God never tires of hearing those who are coming to Him with the things that concern Him. Apart from all the persons who are interceding, God has set up some to be on a constant watch. Although, all are called in Scriptures to "watch and pray" (Mark 13:33; Luke 21:36), these persons are set upon a wall and watch from a place of advantage in a constant and consistent manner.

There is a type of desperation and urgency in a true "watchman" that makes him have to sound the alarm whenever there is trouble. This really is the essence of who a watchman is. He is employed to raise an alarm when danger approaches or is imminent. Such a watchman will "keep not silence". Regardless of the type of personality or temperament the watchman has, when there is danger, he has to get beyond himself and alert the leaders and the people. In the same way, people with the ministry of intercession have to cry out to God. There is no one type of personality or temperament that all intercessors have, much like in a secular army where the soldiers are not carbon-copies of each other. Intercession sometimes could seem to turn you into another type of person, especially when the Spirit of the Lord comes upon you in prayer and you move outside of the realm of self in order to pray what is on God's heart, being led by the Holy Spirit.

The watchman has the affirmation and confidence that his cries won't go in vain because God never becomes weary and wants to stop hearing from him.

THEIR DUTY: WATCHFULNESS; PROTECTION; UNITY; SACRIFICE; PERSEVERANCE

The watchman is always **on the watch for enemy forces** who are sent against the "King" or anything that will act against the welfare of the kingdom (11 Samuel 18:24 – 25). This was so in Bible days and it still is the duty now of every watchman-intercessor, to guard the things of God. This means that if any enemy force slips into the Church unnoticed, the intercessors are also to be held accountable, not just the pastors. When Nehemiah was rebuilding the walls of Jerusalem, the watchman was by his side ready to blow the trumpet at his bidding (Neh. 4:18, 20). So too Church leaders and other leaders should have a watchman-intercessor by his or her side. One who can be trusted to sound an alarm for prayer and to quickly gather the praying troupes within the Church or organization.

It is necessary that the watchman be on another level because the nature of his duty demands that he cannot watch from the same level with everyone else. He has to be watching from a place of advantage (11 Kings 9:17; Isa. 21:6). This is why the intercessor cannot afford to be distracted by the things that easily beset others. God gives intercessors the grace to have anointed eyes to see and ears to hear consistently what is happening around them. The Enemy cannot easily slip by an intercessor whose focus is "watchfulness". This higher place of watchfulness does not mean that the intercessor is above others. His place of advantage is over the Enemy.

Satan is aware of this, so one of his consistent assignments against an intercessor is distraction – by whatever means and using whoever and whatever he can to distract. One can see a perfect example of this in the life of a great intercessor, Nehemiah. As Nehemiah set himself to rebuild the walls of Jerusalem, the enemy forces were relentless to get him to leave what he was called to do. There were at least six strategies that were employed: openly despising the builders (4:1-3); a plot to fight them to cause injury, confusion and failure (4:7-8, 11-13); a call to meetings four times (vs 2-4); the use of propaganda letters (5-9, 17-19); the use of a religious tactic (10-13); and the use of the religious office of the prophets (v. 14).

Nehemiah's response is the response that should come from each intercessor when being tempted and provoked by the Enemy - "I am doing a great work, so that I cannot come down." (Neh 6: 2-3 - ASV). Nehemiah however employed strategies that could instruct intercessors in how to respond to the taunts, haunts and flaunts of the Enemy:

- Continuous Prayer (day and night prayer chain if necessary) while sustaining a heart and mind to continue to do what God has called you to do (4:4-6, 17; Isa. 62:6-7).

- More protection in the weakest areas (4:13, 14). This includes the intercessors' areas of weakness, family members who are most vulnerable and the intercessors who are novices.

- Dealing with fear in our lives which could weaken us in our battle against the Enemy (4:14).

- Ensuring that our hands are innocent regarding injustice (5:7, 11-12, 15).

- All glory goes to God. (6:16).

Another duty of an intercessor is *to protect* as opposed to attacking others. For many intercessors, it is not easy having to live primarily in "war zone" donning combat garments for a long time, then to come out and act completely different. Some have not acquired the necessary skill to know when to fight Satan and at the same time protect others. Sometimes intercessors hurt others by their harsh words, unwise prayers and unloving acts. There are persons within and outside of the Church who have become intimidated by and some fearful of intercessors. This should not be the reaction of those who should be feeling, instead, safely guarded by the intercessor. This problem was found in watchmen in the Old Testament era - they were actually abusive! In Songs of Solomon 5:7, the watchmen smote the woman, wounded her and took her veil from her. This is not a good commentary. May God's watchmen be so groomed, that in my husband, Devon's words, which he often uses to challenge men, may intercessors "be lions when an attack is coming against the family but lambs when interacting within the family and caring for family members."

Having been involved with intercession for over three decades, I have seen within myself and others who carry the ministry of the "watchmen", behaviours that disturbed pastors and others to whom we were submitted. Some of these included spiritual blackmail, deception, divisiveness, entitlement, rebellion and a pharisaical approach. The intercessor should provide protection and Church leaders, members and even those outside of the Church should have confidence in them.

One way to build this confidence is to be *a facilitator of unity*. Intercessors are not always united, seeing "eye to eye". Sometimes they fight against each other, undermining each other's ministries. This divisive attitude often spills over into the general Body and wherever those intercessors go, a spirit of contention and confusion follows them.

"The watchmen shall lift up the voice; with the voice together shall they sing; for they shall see eye to eye, when the Lord shall bring again Zion."

(Isaiah 52:8-KJV)

The fact is that not much will be accomplished in intercession no matter how much labour is put into it if the intercessors are not united. The Scripture clearly defines the type of atmosphere God needs for His blessings to flow – when brethren dwell together in unity (Psalm 133). It is the opposite of a blessing that comes forth when we dwell otherwise. The Apostle James warns us that "every evil work" shows up as a result of strife and contention (Jas 3:14 – 16).

One reason given for some avoiding the act, call and ministry of intercession is the **sacrifice** that it demands. This sacrifice often goes unnoticed, is curtly demanded, oftentimes unappreciated and sometimes backfires, in the sense that an attack is launched against the intercessor by the very person for whom the sacrifice is made. In the following chapter this will be mentioned in more details. Suffice it to say here, that if the intercessor is not constantly aware of Who called him to be a watchman and therefore Who will be rewarding him in the end, he may allow offences to wound his heart. This could weaken him in his ability to intercede, especially for the offending party.

It does demand sacrifice and this is a divinely-inspired sacrifice. It is waking up at any time of the morning or night to pray when the Holy Spirit bids you to; it is coming apart for hours, maybe even days or weeks, for the sole purpose of intercession. This might be while other pleasurable activities are going on of which you desired to be a part. It is having to give up certain habits and indulgences which might not be sinful within themselves, e.g. having a glass of wine, but the Holy Spirit might indicate to the intercessor, using the words of a former Church Elder, "Others might; you can't." It is saying no when you would rather say yes and vise versa. So there have been the missed beach trips going out with the guys or girls, the missed country rides, feting, television-watching and other pleasurable events for the sake of standing-in-the-gap, at a critical time when someone or a nation might need you.

I can recall as a young adult, having tickets for a Barbecue which I was looking forward to attending with my friends. On the day of the Barbecue, I distinctly heard a voice say, "You will not be going to that Barbecue." I knew that voice since I was 15 years old, when I was saved. I submitted and gave up the tickets. I was led to visit an older Church sister's house. When I arrived, she opened the door with her eyes very red from crying. "Did you hear me scream?" she asked. I responded in the negative. She ushered me inside and told me of her ordeal. She was a returning resident and had just wrapped up the final sale of her furniture in the USA. She had about US$3000.00 in her handbag and out of the kindness of her heart, had picked up a young man who was begging a lift. When she dropped him off and checked her handbag upon arriving home a few minutes after, the money was gone.

She was traumatized and almost went berserk! This was all the money she had and was about to invest it as a form of income. I realized, after spending hours with this sister, the reason why I had to sacrifice the Barbeque. It was to be there to comfort a distraught soul and to express God's love for her in spite of. She tangibly experienced God's care, as she expressed to others afterwards, by Him sending someone to pray and be with her during her trauma. Was I happy that I obeyed and made the sacrifice? Oh yes.

This leads to the all-important duty in the intercessor's life, **perseverance**. This perseverance is mostly challenged when the intercessor does his/her duty of sounding the alarm, alerting the people and then is ignored. Jeremiah was a prophet-intercessor who was discouraged to the point of refusing to open his mouth (Jer. 20:8-9). God warned him before, however, as he warns the modern-day intercessors that there are persons who will not care to hear what He is saying or what He is desirous of doing (Jeremiah 6:17). We cannot afford to take this rejection personally.

God's words of comfort to another prophet-intercessor, Samuel, will have to be the intercessors' during this time, "They have not rejected you but they have rejected Me, that I should not be King over them." (I Sam. 8:7).

While going through one of the valleys in my life, being gossiped about, accused of wrongdoing, lied on and abused in different ways, my ministry was being affected. I seriously had to ask God if He had really called me if such things were happening to me. A senior minister encouraged me to leave the island for a while, maybe six months. This was someone who I respected so I prayed and prayed and prayed about his advice. The more I prayed the more the questions kept coming. Why should I run away? What would I do in another land for six months? What would be the purpose to fulfill there? What would change while I was overseas preparing to return? I could not settle and be at peace. As the days went on I knew this was not the way to go. God wanted me to persevere under this trial. I discovered that Satan wanted me out of the way. As one minister said when the trial was over, "This was not about you. It was about destroying the ministry of intercession." This was my perspective too. We are only important to satanic forces if we are an asset or a threat to them. Every day of our lives, we should be a threat!

Another reason the intercessor needs to persevere is that although God has given His watchmen responsibility to watch and to warn, their voices are not always heeded. Intercessors do not have to "fight" others to get them to listen. God will deal with those who refuse to hear Him through whomever He wishes to speak. The intercessor does not pray for revenge upon those who do not listen but he/she prays for mercy, while persevering in praying for God's kingdom to come and His will to be done. He must remain in a place where he can hear from God as he prays and say exactly what God tells him to say (Ezekiel 3:17).

MY OWN STORY

There were some events that solidified my call to the ministry of intercession. This was after I had been involved in intercession for a few years. The first occasion occurred when I was a student attending an all-night prayer meeting. The leader, under the anointing of the Holy Spirit, told me that the Lord had indicated to him that I was "going through struggles but would come out with tremendous joy"; and that God's desire for me was to be broken so that He could implant His very character in me. My challenge was to "learn to yield to the Spirit of God". I interpreted all of that to mean that prayer and intercession was the best place to remain for God to accomplish this complete work in me. I continued attending all the prayer meetings, even attending All-night prayer meetings on Friday nights after working all day and going to a 3-hour class in the evenings. Somehow God gave me the strength to be faithful.

The next occasion came while I was listening to a missionary from the US who was addressing the audience at a Prayer Conference. He shared his struggle with God, asking Him why He had uprooted him and his family to come to Jamaica to stand in-the-gap when there were so many Christians and Churches in the country. He obviously would have preferred to be back home or at least somewhere else where he deemed the need was greater. While I empathized with this man's struggle, I was challenged. A deep conviction resonated in me: "Never again, must I hear these words coming from a foreigner when I am here as a Jamaican." I began to meditate on the missionary's words and quietly thought of how I could bear this mantle. The thought stayed with me for weeks! I later enquired about this speaker and was told that he had returned home. I had a sense that he was released to return home because God had found someone, whether I was that person or another, to fill that gap! I continued walking as an intercessor.

My full call came however at an intercessors' retreat in Jamaica, March 17-20, 1990. Esther Ilnisky was the guest speaker. I was called with a few other leaders to a meeting on the first night in which we were asked to assist in ministry the following morning. I left the meeting disturbed and wondering why I was included because only hours before coming to the retreat I was battling with God; not feeling worthy; tired of my struggles with the flesh; disappointed that I had not had some breakthroughs, especially in my mind, which I had been asking God to do for years. I did not feel prepared in any way to assist but something inside kept telling me not to run away; instead, to just keep talking to God and being truthful as I had been. The following morning, Esther called us back together. I felt a little more settled as I had gotten up early to walk the grounds and talk with God.

Esther asked me to go to the general meeting area where the others were and ask them to "be on their faces before God". When I got to the doorway, the persons in the room were on the floor, praying and crying out to God; no one leading them. I was flabbergasted. I could only return and report that they were already doing that. The morning's session started shortly after and Esther did her usual "Do And Teach" session on intercession. At a particular point in the meeting she stopped and asked us to keep declaring "Freedom". We declared it repeatedly. Suddenly, something hit me. The Holy Spirit came upon me and I felt like a drunken man! No kidding...rocking and stumbling but not falling.

When all this 'strange' feeling was over, apart from feeling physically weak, I felt the consuming fire of God all over me and it stayed with me for a long time. Only a little sleep brought some relief. I felt a brand new person by evening and I **knew** that God had called me into full-time ministry and in particular, full-time intercession. From that day onwards, for over two decades, I have experienced "revival fires" to different degrees at various times. I followed through in obedience to that call by taking a four month leave from my job as a Guidance Counsellor to sit under Esther's mentorship. While there, three weeks prior to my return, the National Intercessory Prayer Network of Jamaica (NIPNOJ) was birthed.

When I returned to my job, I knew I would not be there for long and resigned six months after to take up a position that was created for me at NIPNOJ. I had to find my own support since this was a fledgling ministry. This journey began for me in August 1991. The miracles of support started way back then and in that very month, while being consecrated to my new task at an Intercessors' Conference, I was asked to see backstage, the speaker and his wife who were visiting from overseas. To my surprise, they offered me US$1,000.00 to start my ministry, an offering which they had taken up months before at an Intercessors' gathering in their country. The Lord had revealed to them while I was being presented, that this was the way the offering was to be used. I was humbled. I knew the confirmation of the call was there. I was not going to renege on God. I was launching out into a new ministry; a path I had never taken before. A path that had high points and low points personally and within the ministry but one thing I can never discount and that is God's faithfulness!

CHAPTER 4

Intercession: Dangers and Protection

Men may spurn our appeals, reject our messages, oppose our arguments, despise our persons, but they are helpless against our prayers.

J. Sidlow Baxter

MANY PERSONS SHY away from getting involved in intercession, especially at a deep level, because of **fear**. Fear of what harm might come to anyone who dares to challenge the devil in combative spiritual warfare. They become afraid of his revengeful and retaliatory strategies and scare tactics when his kingdom is disturbed and looted by anyone. I had to face this fact very early in the practice of intercession. This enemy-revenge, however, starts long before one answers the call of being a watchman-intercessor but intensifies the deeper you get into spiritual warfare. The fact is, from the moment the sinner answers the call to follow Christ as a true disciple, the war begins! It is constant fight for the soul of that individual. It is an endless engagement between the flesh and the spirit, God's will and ours, holy angels and demonic entities; a powerful darkness attempting to overcome the light.

Although there are dangers in any warfare, be it in the natural or spiritual, and the intercessor might be exposed to additional dangers that come with the territory, our Commander in Chief, Jesus Christ, has given us certain principles in His Word, that if we adhere to them, we can cut down on casualties and avoid being destroyed in the midst of battle. Some casualties in spiritual warfare have been as a consequence of ignorance.

In Luke 11:4, Jesus taught us to pray, "Lead us NOT into temptation but deliver us from evil / the Evil One. What is evil? It is something hurtful in **effect** or **influence**; morally it is mischief, guilt, malice, the devil. The prayer is a request for Jesus not to permit us to be overcome by evil but deliver us from the Evil One and his influence or effect upon us. This evil needs to be explained specifically for the intercessor and how he should work to avoid this.

Dangers

When you enter the Enemy's camp, you can get hurt! Most times we do get hurt when we are ignorant of his devices.

"Lest Satan should get an advantage of us; for we are not ignorant of his devices."

(11 Cor. 2:11- KJV)

I must confess that on many occasions and especially in my earlier days as an intercessor I was ignorant of Satan's strategies against God's people and in particular those of us who were engaging him in spiritual warfare. Some of his strategies are internal, that is, using the individual's weaknesses to trip him/her up and some are external, attacking the intercessor from the outside by using objects or people. Here are some of Satan's strategies about which we must be on full alert.

One device that Satan uses which endangers the intercessor is **rebellion** which oftentimes comes with a **proud spirit**. This was the reason for Satan's downfall and will cause the watchman- intercessor to run "shipwrecked" every time! Pride and rebellion as shown in the Scriptures, is Satan's very nature (Isa. 14:13-17 and Ezekiel 28:12-18). There are several ways which pride and rebellion show up in the intercessor. Pride can come from seeing answers to prayers manifested either in quick sequences or in an obviously significant manner in, for example, the nation. It is not impossible for an intercessor to pray about a national issue, like the capture of a known criminal, and to see the headlines the following day, announcing his arrest. This, if the intercessor has not learnt who is to get the glory for answered prayers, can begin to think, "I did this. It was my prayers that made them capture him." The truth is, not being omniscient, we do not know who else was praying; which prayer, if any in particular, moved God's heart; and even if that intercessor was the only one who prayed, God should get the glory every time for answers to prayers.

Intercessors, as a result of spending more time than ordinary, in the presence of God, have had some of the experiences that Paul speaks of: mighty visitations, even of angels; powerful dreams and visions oftentimes fulfilled immediately or those that take you into unknown territory bringing revelation of various activities; supernatural experiences that are not normal for the body; the place where they are praying physically shaking, and the list goes on. If these experiences are not taken within the context that a mighty God chooses to visit unworthy men and to reveal Himself to them in various ways; that a supernatural Being chooses to empower mortal lives, then we will not truly understand that such experiences are to further bring us into humility, a falling on our faces before Him, saying, "Only You are worthy." (Revelation 4:11; 5:12-14).

For some reason, there has been a tug o' war for many intercessors to submit to God's delegated authority in the Church. Pastors and other Church leaders have felt this contest for power; a struggle of who is hearing God more; a sense that there are two or more heads in the fellowship while he is the designated shepherd; a 'know-it-all, can't tell me what to do, I only listen to God' type of mentality which is absolutely unbiblical and unchristian. I have seen the results of this attitude of such intercessors who continue to rebel even after being warned by other intercessors – Satan targets them for vicious attacks and there is no spiritual covering so they are naked to the exploits and harassment of the Enemy. Some have been wounded and have never returned to the place of ministry. Some have backslidden and fallen into deception. Pride is a vice. Rebellion is a trap of the Enemy in the intercessors' life.

Another internal problem that the intercessor can have leading him to endangering himself is having a closed spirit. This is a "knowit-all", "cannot-be-taught" attitude which is also a form of pride. Job 36:10 says, "He openeth also their ear to discipline" (KJV). This type of discipline is translated as "saving the mind". He causes them to be open to instruction and correction which will ultimately save them. One of the myths that intercessors should not have is the belief that he/she cannot be deceived. Of course, by virtue of believing this lie, one would have already been deceived. The Scripture states it clearly that God has placed others over us to watch over our souls and they have to give an account to God for us. (Hebrews 13:17). Not only that but we are exhorted to allow them to be able to do so joyfully. This unteachable attitude has caused Church leaders much pain and this is not pleasing to God and it is "not profitable to us" as the Scripture puts it.

Sometimes the people for whom you are praying can be used by the devil to maliciously attack you but one danger is not knowing how to deal with interpersonal conflicts in a Christ-like manner. This is the danger of **unforgiveness and revenge**. Two sister-vices that have led to the downfall of many. Intercession can leave your spirit wide open for offences. If you are regularly in the presence of God praying, your heart becomes in some ways vulnerable to those around you, especially loved ones, ministry partners and those in authority over you. It is not unlikely, that immediately after coming off the mountain top in prayer, for one to encounter an assault through criticism, accusation or persecution. If one is not alert and prepared for the strategies of the Enemy, this can deal a fatal blow to the heart. If the intercessor does not quickly and aptly deal with this wound, it could grow into a cancer within the soul and the pipeline of prayer becomes clogged, rendering any further prayers on behalf of others useless (Matt. 6:14-15; Luke 6:37). This would be more than unfortunate as the role of the intercessor is to be able to offer effectual fervent prayer from a righteous heart that will avail much (James 5:16).

A dangerous practice which is overlooked by many and not heard in many sermons is **presumptiousness in our dealings with the Enemy**. This is being too forward; taking too much for granted; showing overconfidence, arrogance, or effrontery. The Scripture does warn against this and exhorts us concerning a right attitude even in spiritual confrontation with him.

"Yet Michael the archangel, when contending with the devil he disputed about the body of Moses, did not bring against him a railing accusation, but said, The Lord rebuke thee."

(Jude 1:9-KJV)

If even the angels are careful to stand only in the authority of Jesus Christ and never in the flesh to rebuke the devil, should we do less? Intercessors, many times out of lack of teaching, have given the Enemy, as we would say in Jamaica, a "good cussing off", using language that is carnal and definitely lacking the power to move the Enemy. The type of confrontation that would be taken into a "flesh and blood" combat. Ephesians 6:10 warns us that our battle is not against flesh and blood and though we wrestle, it is against wicked spiritual forces which we are told must be fought with spiritual weaponry (11 Cor. 10:4). The bible gives us an account of a set of persons with such misgivings and the consequences that resulted. They were the seven sons of Sceva, the high priest. They tried to exercise authority over the devil that had possessed someone. They obviously did not have the right connection with Jesus and should not have proceeded presumptuously to confront the spirits. These spirits attacked them and they fled naked and wounded from the house (Acts 19:14-16). This is not to scare Christians away from interceding to set men free but rather to instruct us to go, remain, practice and conclude all our dealings regarding the Enemy in the name of the Lord.

In 1987, a spirit of intercession was released upon a church. The leading intercessor, Esther Ilnisky (Esther Network International, USA), knowing that every time a spirit is released by the Lord, the enemy releases counter/opposing spirits, asked the Lord what was the spirit released by the Enemy. God revealed to them that the opposing spirit to intercession is "*lethargy*". This might sound simple but how many times God's watchmen have attempted to fulfill their duties in prayer and an abnormal drowsiness, great lack of energy, inertness, prolonged and unnatural sleep overtakes them. Pretty much the same as the type of sleepiness that swept over the disciples when they should have been watching in prayer with Jesus (Matt. 26:40, 41).

The intercessor, like anyone else, can become fatigued if he or she has been overworked, not getting enough rest and not exercising or eating well. This state of lethargy however, comes upon the intercessor in spite of fulfilling all of the above. Some have reported that this lethargy has come upon them when their lives are not properly connected to God as a result of sin but for the most part, it is a "heavy sleep" that comes upon the intercessor who was heretofore active but as soon as he begins to pray, he becomes, drunk with sleep.

How is this dangerous? The Scripture makes it clear that the bottom line of any assignment of Satan, whatever spirits he releases is to "steal, kill and destroy". If lethargy comes upon you when you are assigned to pray for someone, for example, who might be facing danger in that moment, when that danger could be averted by prayer, it might not. I have heard so many testimonies from especially parents who have been up in the third and fourth watches of the morning (12:00 – 6:00a.m.) praying for their children upon being awakened and alerted to pray. The result: various testimonies of God's intervention which foiled some criminal intent, a horrible accident which should have led to death, that child coming under serious conviction, having to abort an immoral act.

For some intercessors, lethargy plays out in a sense of total indifference, apathy and forgetfulness. Upon examination, the intercessor is able to identify this state as unnatural and to quickly take action in order to terminate it.

One of the dangers experienced by some intercessors is **the sowing of human agents** in their lives who the Enemy can easily access and use to carry out his demonic assignment, to steal, kill and destroy (John 10:10). Such persons are usually sown in the intercessor's personal life / ministry to further the cause of Satan in his attempt to halt intercession and annihilate intercessors. These persons are experienced as toxic and in the same way that toxins bring harm to the human body, these individuals, influenced by demons, can so poison a ministry that, if God does not intervene and bring deliverance, those ministers and their ministries, will become obsolete. The attacks are usually vicious ranging from slander, false accusations, interruptions in the times of prayer, verbal / physical abuse, competition, witchcraft praying, display of demonically motivated gifts (Acts 8:9-25) and the pursuance of intimate relationships with the intercessors.

The website (*http://www.jwipn.com/pdf/cywtp_chapter32*) outlines for the intercessor some dangers and pitfalls. The writer points out that "We are human and liable to error (fallible) and therefore we should heed the following (Adapted):

- Sometimes an intercessor uses the information he gets to slander ... Gossip is always negative and always has negative consequences.

- Potential sexual danger. The male spiritual worker has to be very careful of any relationship with female intercessors. Don't pray with a female intercessor when the two of you are alone.

- Beware of an Absalom attitude in prayer. This attitude is sometimes found in intercessors. One might feel that one is not given enough credit and then try to force the spiritual worker in the wrong direction through prayer.

- The intercessor should not take over the task of the spiritual worker by trying to manipulate him by soul stirring prayers.

- From the above it becomes clear that it is possible for a power struggle to develop between the intercessor/s and the spiritual worker. The power, leadership and authority to make decisions and lead is given by God to the spiritual worker. The intercessor has missed the mark concerning his calling and commission.

- Along with the Absalom attitude comes "witchcraft" praying. Magic is used to get a person to do what you want him to do. The same can happen to intercessors. For instance: they want the spiritual worker to teach or do something specific in the congregation. To reach their goal they force him into a certain direction through "prayer". Such prayers are done in the flesh and usually do much harm.

Protection

Intercessors have a sure protection from God in spite of the dangers and pitfalls. The Holy Spirit is present in the intercessor's life to teach him/her and will do so directly through the Word and speaking to him/her in various other ways – other people, dreams, visions, prophetic utterances and circumstances. It is therefore critical for the intercessor to note *the helps* that he has been given for intercession to lessen casualties in this ministry.

HELP OF THE HOLY SPIRIT

Romans 8:26 – 28 tells us that "the Spirit also helpeth our infirmities: for we know not what we should pray for as we ought: but the Spirit itself maketh intercession for us."(KJV) Jesus made it very clear that the Holy Spirit is given to us as a Paraclete which means an advocate or helper. Since the arm of flesh cannot fulfil the purposes of God, this Paraclete is sent to teach us all things (John 14:26) and to help us where we are weak. The word 'infirmities" comes from the Greek word, *astheneia* which means, "want of strength", "weakness", indicating inability to produce results. A raw translation of the phrase in Greek is "takes share in the weakness of us". What a precious gift that is given to the Christian and to those who are called to be watchmen-intercessors.

Some possible infirmities/weaknesses could be conscious iniquity of our hearts when we come to pray; ignorance concerning the will of God; physical weakness – infirmity in our bodies, which impact on the "strength" that we need to persevere in prayer and the struggle against Satan who seeks to oppress or depress or to create doubt, disillusionment and discouragement.

The passage enlightens us that "we know not what we should pray for as we ought …" indicating the lack of knowledge and lack of methodology often experienced in prayer. But the Spirit Himself "makes intercession for us with groans that words cannot express." This suggests that there is a level of supplication/intercession that only the Holy Spirit knows how to pray and this is deep in my spirit (without words). There are several theories put forth in order to explain the meaning of "groanings". One theory is that this groaning refers to "praying in tongues". However, tongues is nowhere else described as 'groaning' but more as a language – words spoken.

KJV Dictionary (av1611.com/kjbp/kjv-dictionary/groan.html) defines "groan" as "grunnio; Heb. to cry out, to groan. Which is (i) to breathe with a deep murmuring sound; to utter a mournful voice, as in pain or sorrow. "For we that are in this tabernacle, do groan, being burdened." (2 Cor.5). 2. (ii) to sigh; to be oppressed or afflicted; or to complain of oppression. (iii) GROAN, n. A deep mournful sound, uttered in pain, sorrow or anguish. This type of praying with the Spirit here seems to suggest, a type of praying that utilizes the body, comes deep from the soul of man, but is supernaturally motivated by the Holy Spirit.

One thing is clear: The Spirit links Himself with us in our praying and supports us by pulling from deep within us, the thing that ails us. I can think of times, when I have been in deep agony, often traumatized by experiences – having 24 hours to move out of a rented apartment that was, unknown to us, illegally rented, though we had a rental agreement that was signed and monies paid; at the tragic death of our young son; being misjudged by a Church whose leadership I had served for years. During these times, as much as I had been mentored and had mentored others in praying, no words could come but a deep groaning, as if in physical pain. This emotional pain was too intense to utter in oratorical tones; too deep to form orderly words to express and too laden with mixed emotions to speak forth in a discerning prayer.

K. Hagin in his book, The Art of Prayer, writes: "Sometimes I have tried to pray for people, and it would seem like I run up against a blank wall, or down a blind alley. I just didn't get anywhere because the Spirit of God didn't take hold of me." (p.97).

When the Holy Spirit is energizing and empowering you in praying, you can pray for hours and not feel the natural drain that you would if you were praying dutiful prayers. You pray under divine inspiration, uttering prayers that you know was not coming from your own mind and emotions. It is akin to feeling like a "Superman" or "Superwoman". This is also the reason why God should get all the glory when we pray powerful effectual prayers.

The Holy Spirit also gives us "strategy" for that particular time/ moment of intercession. Not every occasion, as we see in the Old and New Testament in the times of battle, the servants of God prayed the same prayers or were instructed by God to use the same strategy as used before to win in the current situation. Many times in intercession we have to wait for the Holy Spirit to give us a plan in prayer to defeat the Enemy. A strategy therefore is to help us to effectively utilize the weapons of warfare through offensive prayer, destroy the plans of Satan in order to release God's power and influence a given situation. At times the strategy might be going physically to the place to pray, laying of hands, praying with unknown tongues, praying with understanding, utilizing worship at the beginning, end or throughout the time of intercession; using the musical instruments in warfare; praying all night; adding fasting to prayer. Sometimes the strategy the Holy Spirit gives is not delightful to the intercessor, endearing to others or cute in its manifestation. At such times, the intercessor has to be obedient and remind himself or herself that this is not about him/her but about God!

I have been led to do things under the unction of the Holy Spirit that I knew in my mind, I would never dream of doing and certainly would not want anyone to have any misgivings of me by my doing that act. One such occasion was at a prayer meeting in Florida. I was a visitor. They were attempting to deliver a lady from demonic oppression. I stood in intercession, like many others, pleading for a breakthrough. The Holy Spirit spoke to me to jump over her three times. I argued with this Voice. I debated. I tried to speak sense into Him by reminding Him of where I was and who these people were. I was a foreigner; a young person; a novice and not Caucasian.

In the midst of that mental and physical struggle came the voice of my mentor, Esther Ilnisky. "Maria," she spoke through the mike. "Whatever the Lord is telling you to do, do it!" It was a caring command. I decided to instantly obey, trusting that my mentor's words were a confirmation. I stepped towards the woman and jumped over her three times. She let out a shriek, her body shuddered and she was free. The people rejoiced and the woman was in tears, crying out, I am free! What's in three jumps? Maybe nothing more than what was in the dirt that Jesus placed on the blind man's eyes (John 9:6) but one thing we know of Jesus, which should be the position of every strategic intercessor, "I do only what I see the Father doing." (John 5:19, 30).

ROLE OF THE WORD OF GOD

God's will can only be truly known in the watchman-intercessor's life if he/she spends quality time reading the Scriptures which are not only God's love letter to His people but map for life and a manual for how He wants His Kingdom to be set up for His rule. Knowing God's will is not a "spooky" exercise. Much of God's will is already expressed in His word and many times to lead us in specific areas, even to help us to understand biblical and modern-day prophecies, He reminds us of principles from His words. A rule of thumb for the intercessor could be: If it does not line up with the Scriptures then I cannot embrace it and I cannot pray against what God's Word clearly says is to be. One basic example of this is the clear Scriptural references to the coming of the anti-Christ. Even if all the watchmen-intercessors declared a time of fasting and prayer against his coming into the world, he is going to come and those would be wasted prayers and audacious praying. Knowing God's will through His Word can assist the intercessor in not falling into the trap of **presumptuous** praying.

An intercessor who feels he/she has some mysterious 'straight line' to God and does not need His Word is opening up himself/herself to deception and demonic influence. Satan loves to have God's creation in the dark but God's Word brings us into light and it specifically brings the issues of our hearts to light too (Psalm 119:105; John 8:12; I John 1:7). It is interesting to note Jesus' use of the Scriptures even when confronting the Enemy. The question to ask is what if Jesus had not known the Scriptures and their correct application when Satan came to tempt Him? Would that battle have gone on longer than it should? Would Satan have worn Him down and in some way be able to harm Him if He did not know how to skillfully use His sword as part of His offensive weapon against the Enemy? (Ephesians 6:17).

Jesus' response every time the Enemy came to tempt Him in Luke 4:1 – 13 is more than a clue to the type of response that a watchman-intercessor should give when he too is tempted and also as he/she battles for the Kingdom of God. Jesus' answer every time was what the Word of God had to say about the particular situation, in principle. IT IS WRITTEN…!!! Jesus never cussed him, called him names, or treated him with 'fleshly weapons'. Instead he used the Word of God which is "**quick** and **powerful**, **sharper** than any two-edged sword… **piercing**…" (Hebrews 4:12). Such potent words to describe the tool and weapon that we have with which to fight.

For effective prayers to happen, we must also know how to pray the Word of God. We can actually pray the Scriptures. For example, the intercessor who wants to pray for another believer and does not know how to pray would not miss by praying the Word. Two Scriptures that are apt in this regard are Ephesians 1:15 –19 and Colossians 1:9 – 12.

"Therefore I also, after I heard of your faith in the Lord Jesus and your love for all the saints, 16 do not cease to give thanks for you, making mention of you in my prayers: 17 that the God of our Lord Jesus Christ, the Father of glory, may give to you the spirit of wisdom and revelation in the knowledge of Him, 18 the eyes of your understanding[a] being enlightened; that you may know what is the hope of His calling, what are the riches of the glory of His inheritance in the saints, 19 and what is the

exceeding greatness of His power toward us who believe, according to the working of His mighty power."

(Ephesians 1:15-19 - NKJV)

One thing that should be noted from Luke 4:1-13 where the devil came to tempt Jesus is that the devil also knows the Word of God and will try to deceive us using that very word. This is all the more reason why every intercessor should meditate on and activate the Word of God in his/her life and carry it especially in the heart, as a tool of his/her trade. Jude 8, 9 - no railings against Satan.

DAILY COVERING

An intercessor, like a security guard or a sentinel in the natural, must have some form of clothing or weaponry to protect him. The Scriptures outline ways in which the watchman-intercessor can cover himself daily as he operates in his position. The list of his armor is given in Ephesians 6:10-13. The Christian is exhorted to "Put on the whole armor of God, that ye may be able to stand against the wiles of the devil." (6:11- KJV). The pieces are outlined for us perhaps to ensure that no one misses any since they work together to form an accurate and suitable defense system. They are:

- helmet of salvation which covers the mind

- breastplate of righteousness which has to do with right relationship with God and man.

- loins girt about with truth noting a covering of one's private and re- productive areas

- feet shod with the preparation of the gospel of peace which is specifically addressing how we walk through life; where we go; what we walk with (the Gospel)

- shield of faith addressing the fact that the Christian life cannot be lived without this and we will not accomplish what pleases God if we don't have it (Heb. 11:6)

- sword of the spirit, the Word of God, our offensive weaponry

It is crucial that intercessors cover each other in prayer. An intercessor can know when he/she is not being covered. Somehow the attacks come differently and one has a feeling of being very "exposed" as if without defense. At those times, the intercessor can cry out to God to have someone cover him/her and to ask God to help him/her to choose persons who could and would faithfully be "watching their backs".

There have been times when I have felt this exposure to the Enemy and a sense that I am not covered. When I cried to the Lord for His covering, I sensed when it came. Interestingly, many times I found out weeks after the fact, when someone, usually an acquaintance, informs me that God had placed me heavily in their spirit and has had them praying for me. Some have made several long-distance calls to find out what is going on why they have had such a burden for me. What a God? Thanks to those who will hear and obey God. We do not know on this side of heaven how the story could have turned had it not been for obedient intercessors!

SUBMISSION AND HUMILITY

A submissive attitude and a teachable spirit are such explosive weapons in the intercessor's hand that if he realizes this, he would groom his life to make it a part of his daily adornment. A holy and submissive life is one weapon that the Enemy cannot resist. Why this in particular? Satan's downfall is rebellion. He hates anything that opposes his nature. In the same way that love is a weapon against hate. It is important to note that even if we use all the other weapons of warfare listed above, if we are not submissive, we open ourselves to serious attacks. The warfare-intercessor in particular, cannot afford to leave himself/herself open to unnecessary attacks. This is one guarantee that the Scripture gives that will make the devil flee! Jesus' use of the Word in Luke 4 which led to his victory over Satan came also with a submissive attitude to His Father.

> *"Submit yourselves therefore to God. Resist the devil, and he will flee from you."*

> *(James 4:7, 8 KJV)*

Submission precedes resistance and the ultimate goal, the devil fleeing from the intercessor.

RIGHT RELATIONSHIPS

Since relationships can make us or break us, and since the Enemy will be attempting to sow persons in the lives of the intercessor to destroy the latter's ministry, then it is incumbent on the watchman-intercessor to discerningly choose the right persons with whom to have intimate relationships. It might be a good rule of thumb to ask the Lord, who knows the hearts of men, including the intercessor's heart, to provide **divine connections** among the people we meet. This is one surety for the intercessor – when God chooses. God's choice might not be the persons with whom one might have felt an affinity, but as the relationship unfolds, God will also reveal His purpose for the connection. As the intercessor matures, he will discover that, as God revealed to the intercessor-prophet Samuel, outward appearances can fool even the best of persons. It is God Who looks at the heart (I Samuel 16:6, 7).

Another feature of relationships that can be a protection for the watchman-intercessor is the right or righteous handling of them. It is a disposition that is **quick-to-forgive** and keeps-**short-records-of-wrongs** that works for the intercessor in marriage and family life, in relationships within and outside of the Body of Christ. There is one finger that the Enemy should never be able to point at the intercessor and be right, and that is the accusation that he or she is unforgiving and full of malice. The Scripture is replete with principles, directives and commands about how we ought to relate to others and the **foundation of all relationships should be love** (Mark 11:25; I Corinthians 13; Ephesians 4:2; I John 3:16-18). One type of relationship that the watchman-intercessor can never afford is to be unequally yoked (II Cor. 6:14-18). If the Enemy can sow a believer into our lives and use his/her weaknesses to trip us up in ministry, even more so, when he has full access to one who is a stranger to the Kingdom of God.

THE SPIRIT OF A WARRIOR

The spirit of a **warrior/soldier**. "Intercession is not for 'paper soldiers'." Those who stand in their position as watchmen-intercessors cannot be tangled up in civilian affairs (2 Tim. 2:4). As the Holy Spirit galvanizes him for battle, he must be prepared to advance on the Camp of the Enemy and to take back all that Satan has stolen. This is no child's play and certainly not for a boot-camper who has not learnt the art of combat and the posture of confrontation. The intercessor has to understand and be willing to advance the Kingdom of God by fulfilling Matthew 11:12:

> *"And from the days of John the Baptist until now the kingdom of heaven suffereth violence, and the violent take it by force."*

> *(KJV)*

Esther Ilnisky puts it this way:

'Intercession is violence! It is one of the most intense exercises of the Church and it takes dedicated, determined, sanctified, aware, alert, Spirit-energized people to engage in it! It is our highest form of response to the admonition: "…..the Kingdom of heaven suffers violence and the violent take it by force." Matt.11:12.'

(Esther Ilnisky, Intercessory Prayer Workshop I, ENI, 1989)

I can remember having to learn this to save my mind. While a student at the Caribbean Graduate School of Theology in Jamaica, I was facing intense witchcraft. Satan was using a neighbour who wanted the bigger flat that my room-mate and I was renting. This was not superstition, suspicion or conjecture. We caught her and her son one night lighting a fire at our steps and heard their evil conversation. We were returning home from a cell group meeting and were not easily seen because there was a power-cut. As soon as we were spotted, the fire was quickly put out. We entered our home with much prayer.

The lights came back to reveal liquid and powder splattered and sprinkled all over our verandah, and on both front doors. We immediately began with loud prayers to declare the Scriptures of warfare – that no weapon formed against us (Isa. 54:17) would prosper; the weapons of our warfare were not carnal (2 Cor. 10:4); they overcame him by the blood of the Lamb (Rev. 12:11) and so on. We had the victory. A few weeks after however, a couple who had joined forces with our neighbour to fight against us, came under serious attack. The woman became very ill and we had to intercede for her life! Thank God that her life was spared and she and her "common-law" spouse later became Christians.

Some months after this, my mind came under severe attack. I was on campus and felt as if, to use an expression, I was "checking out and checking in". I could not focus. I knew it was a spiritual attack and went in search for someone to pray with me. I visited a friend who was living on campus and she and another guest present prayed a simple devotional prayer that did not move anything. I knew I had to find an intercessor and one who knew warfare praying! After summoning this person, a fellow student and friend, she ushered me into her dorm-room and began to do spiritual warfare. I could feel things crumbling even within my stomach. She encouraged me not to leave her room but to remain for the night until I was fully recovered. She returned to her studies in the library but I knew that she was watching over me in prayer. The next morning I was fine. I have never forgotten that incident and the lessons learnt from the spirit of that warrior.

THE RIGHT WAY TO END INTERCESSION

After a period of intercession, our focus should be turned towards God (in worship) and we should continue our daily walk of intimacy with Him. There is no victory and no mountain top experience that can replace the rigours and pleasures of a daily walk with the greatest intercessor, Jesus. Having fought in prayer with the forces of darkness, our time of prayer, be it personal or corporate should end with us focusing our attention on God. Worship, giving God thanks and recommitting our lives to His service are some ways that we can refocus.

The watchmen-intercessors should pray against any spirit of revenge or retaliation against them, their families, ministries, etc. especially when the Enemy has been engaged in spiritual warfare. One declaration that I often make over myself and others engaged along with me in warfare comes from Psalm 23:6 – only goodness and mercy will follow me. I usually declare that none of the spirits that were dealt with will follow any of us, torment any of us or in any way harm us, our families, ministries, even our acquaintances. The benediction is usually done to release God's blessings upon His warriors (Numbers 6:24-26).

I would not want to end this section without sharing the story of another general of intercession. He is founder of the National Intercessory Prayer Network of Jamaica and Founder and President of the Intercessory Prayer Ministry International. He was my local mentor in intercession in the foundation and the inauguration of the establishment of my ministry and has spoken words from the Lord into my life which were fulfilled. Here is his personal account of dangers and protection in the intercessors life.

NEWTON GABBIDON'S STORY

Intercessory Prayer Ministry International (IPMI) was established in 1996 in Brooklyn, NY from a small prayer group comprising primarily of Jamaican Christians from New York City, Long Island and New Jersey that had been meeting in a home to pray for revival. About two years after that, one of our daughters, who was then in high school, became rebellious to the point of becoming demonized. This posed a major challenge not only for the family trying to cope with the full impact of her rebellion, but for me and the viability of IPMI, which had become the primary target of her disaffection. For the two years that the experience lasted, not only did I become spiritually exhausted, having explored all options of getting help for our daughter, including counseling and prayer support; but I had reached the point of complete discouragement and at one point, considered walking away from the ministry. As far as I was concerned, I had failed desperately in my role as the spiritual head of my household and therefore, was no longer qualified to lead IPMI.

Since its inception, IPMI, has hosted an annual 21 days of prayer and fasting for breakthrough between September and October. This has been a very successful program based on the number of testimonies we have received over the years from participants around the world. In September 2000, I became totally desperate and decided to dedicate the entire 21 days of prayer and fasting for the breakthrough of our daughter. By this time, she was attending college in New York City as a freshman. As part of my preparation for this period of prayer and fasting, I decided to research the Scriptures to re-examine God's plans and purposes for the children of His people. This exercise completely convinced me that it was God's will to save, protect, deliver and prosper the children of His people. I also became convinced that God would intervene in my own situation with my daughter through the power of prayer and fasting. With this in mind, I completed a list of pertinent Scriptures involving God's promises to bless, deliver and prosper the children of the righteous, including such verses as "the seed of the righteous shall be delivered" and "the seed of the righteous shall be mighty upon the land." For nineteen days I prayed for my daughter, declaring this list of Scriptures.

On the nineteenth day of the fast, I received a strong sense of assurance from the Holy Spirit that God had heard my prayers and had intervened in her situation. At that point I began to praise God for this amazing victory. Of course, we noticed no immediate change in the situation. This came one month after at the 4th Saturday meeting in November 2000, where she showed up for the first time in over two years of utter rejection of me and IPMI, to seek God for deliverance. The rest is history. She was mightily delivered of the spiritual bondages that held her captive for almost three years. In addition, she fully surrendered her life to the Lord; sought the forgiveness of the family for all the pain and suffering that she caused; and then, she enrolled in a Christian college, to pursue God's plan and purpose for her life.

The experience of her deliverance has not only resulted in a number of her schoolmates coming to Christ but wherever the testimony was shared it resulted in the spiritual encouragement of many.

I learned a number of lessons, which I outlined in my 2012 Schools of Prayer Series on Spiritual Warfare and Intercession, which are important for persons already engaged in, or planning to become engaged in any type of spiritual ministry. Here are just a few of these lessons:

1. Satan's primary mission is to oppose God and His people. At the very heart of this primary mission is to frustrate God's purposes in the lives of God's people. I came to learn that lesson the hard way through this experience that could have caused the loss of my daughter and possibly my family and ministry. But how do we overcome such onslaught of Satan against the purpose of God in our lives? The key is found in Num. 23:19, which says, "God is not a man that He should lie; neither the son of man that He should repent; hath He said, and shall He not do it? Or hath He spoken, and shall not make it good" (KJV). In order to frustrate God's purposes in your life, Satan will do everything in his power to get you to grieve God's heart by doubting His integrity. And that is why during that time of severe testing, it was so important for me to actually spend time reading and assuring myself of the things that God had revealed in His words concerning my seed.

2. Satan seeks to oppose God's purposes in your life because they represent a direct threat to his kingdom on earth. That's the reason behind the death of Christ; that is the reason behind the temptation of Peter: "Simon, Simon, behold, Satan has desired to sift you, that he might sift you as wheat" (Luke 22:31, KJV). But notice the words of Jesus in verse 32: "But I have prayed for thee that thy faith fail not; and when thou art

converted, strengthen thy brethren." The sole purpose of this temptation was to destroy Peter's faith and ultimately prevent the birth of his apostolic ministry.

3. Another very important lesson particularly for intercessors comes from a word of caution shared by Mike Murdock in *Battle Techniques for the War-Weary Saints, 1987*. Murdock cautions that while it is important that we recognize the authority we have in Christ, it is equally important to avoid an attitude of overconfidence. Overconfidence can leave us vulnerable, resulting in us being hurt spiritually, emotionally and physically. For Murdock, the key here for the battle-worn Christian is to be able to predict his/her season of attack. There are at least three such seasons to consider: (i) When you become physically exhausted. Faith and enthusiasm wane through fatigue; (ii) When you face major changes in your life. This may be in your career or with geographical locations. Crisis always occur on the curve of change; (iii) when you make an effort to launch a new ministry for God. Notice that Jesus faced his wilderness experience just prior to his healing ministry.

By now you would have realized that the last two points relate very much to us. Migration to New York City proved a rather challenging experience socially and spiritually for my family and I and it helped set the stage or created the conditions that Satan exploited in his attack against us. And of course, enough was not done defensively in anticipation of such an attack when IPMI was created. Since then however, we have followed proper protocol as much as possible through the establishment of a prayer shield over IPMI and its leaders to guard the ministry against such future attacks.

(Rev. Newton Gabbidon, Founder/President, Intercessory Prayer Ministry International, USA)

A PRAYER FOR COVERING

Magnificent Father. Creator of the whole human race and the One Who is in control in heaven, on earth and over principalities and powers, the rulers of the darkness of this world and spiritual wickedness in high places, according to Ephesians 6:10. We worship You because You alone deserve worship.

We recognize that as children of the Most High God, we have become targets of the realms of darkness and the kingdom of the Evil and Wicked one, whose assignment it is, to steal, kill and destroy, according to John 10:10. We thank you however that according to John 10:10, you have come that we might have life over death and abundance of life over poverty and distress. You came to, on our behalf, destroy the works of the devil (1 John 3:8). This was your mission, your destination and your position when you walked the earth. The recipient was very clear – the devil. We thank You that You continue to destroy His works today so no weapon formed against us shall prosper (Isa. 54:17). We thank you for the angels on assignment who help us to do warfare against the flesh, world and the devil (Psalm 91:12; Heb. 1:14).

As our lives are engaged in spiritual battles, I/we now ask for our armour to be tightly fitted; the covering of your blood; cleansing from any contamination of the kingdom of darkness. I/we declare that only goodness and mercy follow us. None of the spirits that we have dealt with follow us or will torment us, our families, our ministry partners, our Church fellowship, our businesses and workplaces, our communities. Everything that we possess is covered from the least to the greatest. This place where we engaged in warfare is covered and all those who will come after us with no evil intention.

As we leave this place, **only goodness and mercy** will follow us to our residences. *No spirit that has preceded us, will intercept us or will track us along the way. We thank You that heaven backs us and your presence is always with us (Joshua 1:5; Heb. 13:5). Our lives will continue to magnify You and You alone. In Jesus' Name we pray. Amen.*

CHAPTER 5

Prayer...Weapon of Spiritual Warfare

Pray often, for prayer is a shield to the soul, a sacrifice to God, and a scourge for Satan.

John Bunyan

THE TERM SPIRITUAL warfare has been used in the previous chapters and it is necessary before proceeding to chapters which will address specific areas of combat, to properly define this sphere of engagement. Warfare is between two or more enemy forces and has to do with fighting, struggle and combat. This combat is usually aggressive. In the natural, one is familiar with the terms military operations, political warfare, guerrilla warfare and chemical warfare. Usually the intent of the enemy is to undermine the strength of another with the ultimate goal of destroying its opponent. Roget's Thesaurus: Home Library Literature & Language Thesaurus defines warfare as a vying with others for victory or supremacy; a state of open, prolonged fighting and a state of disagreement and disharmony. [Read more: http://www.answers.com/topic/warfare] All of these terms could be applied to the warfare that the Christian is engaged in except that this warfare is not fleshly, carnal or between humans; it is spiritual in nature and sphere, that is where this battle takes place.

Ephesians 6:12 is one of the signatory Scriptures for those wielding weapons in a spiritual war. It clearly informs us that "we wrestle not against flesh and blood, but against **principalities**, against **powers**, against the **rulers** of the darkness of this world, against **spiritual wickedness** in high places."(KJV) These are obviously categories, degrees and scopes of this warfare pointing to various ranks within the Enemy's domain. Reminding ourselves that Satan and his demonic forces were angels who were once serving with God, it would not be incredulous to think of them as keeping basically a similar ranking as they did before they had fallen since God's holy angels are placed in ranks – the Bible mentions seraphim, cherubim, thrones, dominions, principalities, powers and archangels (Ezekiel 1:4-28, 10:3-22; Colossians 1:16; Rev. 4:7, 8). New King James Version puts it this way: "For we do not wrestle against flesh and blood, but against principalities, against powers, against the rulers of the darkness of this age, against spiritual *hosts* of wickedness in the heavenly *places*." (Eph 6:12)

There are two accounts in Scriptures that vividly outline the warfare in which we are engaged. The first outlines, at least in principle, how we should approach this warfare. This is the account of David in Ziklag, Philistine territory (1 Samuel 30). Having left Ziklag for three days, upon David and his army of 600 men's return, Ziklag was burnt to the ground by their enemies and their families were taken captive. David engaged himself in a manner that was exemplary and is instructive for those who engage in spiritual battles. Upon discovering this great loss, he was struck to the core in a similar way that any human would when facing trauma and tragedy. He however, did not allow his loss to become a distraction for too long. David did the following:

- He encouraged and strengthened himself in the Lord (v 6)

- He enquired of the Lord the steps he should take (v 8)

- God's Instructions: Pursue; overtake; recover all (v 8)

- He obeyed God's instructions and found victory (vs 18. 19)

- Acknowledged Who gave him victory over his enemies (v 23)

- Those who stay behind (if it is even to watch and pray) are worthy of recognition as those who are on the frontline in battle (v 24)

- Whatever was his as a part of his victory he shared (v 26)

The instructions to pursue, overtake and recover all could sum up what the engagement of watchmen-intercessors do in spiritual warfare. The intercessor is in an offensive mode, not backing down from the Enemy but pursuing, being persistent knowing that the battle might not be won in a short period. If all the intercessor did was to pursue the Enemy then not much would be accomplished. The next strategy is to know how to overtake him and to bind the strongman who is armed to keep his wares and to never let it go from him (Mark 3:27; Luke 11:21). Luke 11:22 reminds us that there is a stronger person who can come to displace him! Here are a few ways that one can engage oneself in binding the strongman and taking back all that he has stolen.

Firstly, we need to do warfare over our own lives until everything in us comes under captivity to Christ (11 Cor. 10: 4 – 6). Confession and Repentance in prayer is very powerful when we are engaged in spiritual warfare (Nehemiah 1:4 – 6). If the watchman-intercessor is practicing sin, he is fuelling the camp of the Enemy and "how can Satan cast out Satan?" (Mark 3: 23 - ASV). Sin in the intercessor's life, quenches the work and power of the Holy Spirit, and this power is what is needed, not our own strength, to bind the strongman.

Secondly, when opposition comes directly from the Enemy or is instigated by the Enemy through others, we oppose first with prayer. Praying during warfare and opposition gives one God's STRATEGY to fight the Enemy (Nehemiah 4:1 - 9).

Thirdly, we cannot afford to "come down" from the stance of prayer and warfare to debate with the Enemy (Nehemiah 6: 2 – 5). The devil always recognizes a HOLY and SUBMITTED life because therein lies authority (Jas 4: 7, 8)! When we stay in the place of prayer in warfare and win, God takes pleasure in spreading the table before us in the presence of our enemies (Nehemiah 6:15f.).

Another account in Scripture that enlightens us concerning what to do in spiritual warfare is the account of our Lord facing Satan in the wilderness (Luke 4). Here are some principles that can be gleaned from this passage. Knowledge of the Word of God is critical as this is the offensive part of the armour needed to protect the watchman-intercessor in battle. Knowing how, when and where to apply this knowledge is expedient as Satan also knows the Scriptures and has used Scriptures himself to deceive many. This skill in application comes by asking God for wisdom from above even as we walk through the Scriptures. It should be noted that every aspect of Jesus' existence was tested: He was first tempted in the area of his appetite (Luke 4:3, 4). This is an area that the watchman-intercessor has to watch over, even while he is in the midst of prayer, fasting and spiritual warfare. This is the realm of the "lust of the flesh". Jesus was then tempted to have Satan / the things of the world as idols. Since the watchman-intercessor has to live in this world, he can be tempted like anyone else to run after the "bling" and things of the world!

I can recall one prayer meeting while in deep intercession, the Lord asking, in a persistent voice which I in turn vocalized, "Where are my intercessors?" He asked about three times and each time I drew a blank! Why was He asking this question? What is the meaning of this? I know that He would enlighten my ignorance. "They are out counting money," was His response. At that point I knew that many who were to be engaged in "watching" had left their posts and were pursuing the wealth of this world in a manner that was displeasing to God. One intercessor, out of this revelation, felt that I should call a meeting of God's people to address some issues that were breaking His heart. A "clarion call" was made. Many came and shared. Many confessed. Many repented, even in the gap, for those who had displeased God. Every watchman-intercessor has to be on the lookout for the pull of the world in whatever area. For those living on low-incomes, their pull might be to "come down" from the wall of the watchman, in order to make more money; it might be to get involved in an illicit relationship which has the potential to advance him/her materially; it could be a fixation in the place of envying others, which would send a statement to God, that one is not content with what He is providing. This is the lust of the eyes (1 John 2:16).

Jesus was also tempted to prove Himself in terms of Who He was and the power He had. This is what the Scripture terms as the pride of life (1 John 2:16). As the watchman-intercessor grows in strength in intercession and begins to see the answers to many of his prayers, he has to be vigilant and aware of that "voice of flattery" that can lead him to feel as if he is the one doing this of himself; he is the best thing ever created; no one can achieve what he has. One antidote, whether in or outside of warfare is to ensure that with every compliment, accolade, promotion or acquisition of wealth, the watchman-intercessor steps up another notch in humility. One songwriter penned this line: "The more God blesses you; the more humble you should be."

Dr. Karl I. Payne in his book, *Spiritual Warfare*, informs his readers that spiritual warfare is real.

The world, the flesh, and the devil represent confrontation in three areas: sociological, physiological, and supernatural... Christians must be strategic in their response to these three enemies, learning how to fight biblically and effectively rather than just sincerely.

(Preface)

Steve Hawthorne, a leading intercessor, did a series of videos on *"Spiritual War is: Wisdom For The Window."* In these videos he explained what spiritual warfare is. This comprehensive teaching on the topic, although he applied much of his teaching to the realm of Prayer Walking, helped me to put some things in perspective in my earlier days of ministry. Hawthorne suggests that spiritual warfare is:

- God **defeating** His enemies and **drawing** all peoples to Christ. John 12:31, 32 - Now is the judgement of this world; now shall the prince of this world be cast out. And I, if I be lifted up from this earth I will draw all men unto me.

- Spiritual war prepares the way for victory by **displacement** of evil by Christ's life rather than by the mere destruction of evil. *Overcome evil with good.

- Spiritual warfare is **authority with Christ** because all authority is given to Him (Matthew 28:18). He points out that this authority.is given, never taken; we express God's authority - not our exaltation; it is guided authority.

» Your discernment will often exceed your authorization to act. You are going to see more evil than God is taking care of through you.

» It is purposeful - it is to be used in prayer in order to draw people to Christ. Matthew 16:19 - Binding is for loosing (liberation of people!)

» Relational authority - Exult in your identity before God in Christ. It's not what you know or who you know but who knows you. (Acts 19:13-17)

» Spiritual warfare is not glorying / having your identity in the place or with the power one has with demons (Luke 10:17 - 20) (*Adapted*)

There was a season in my life when I faced the "hordes of hell". The onslaught came from every angle. It came through human agents. I was armed and ready, in the flesh, to release all the ammunition I had, even about their lives, to destroy them and to stop the "mud-slinging" and the smear campaign against me. I made my tearful and desperate appeal to God regarding the main player. "This person is destroying my reputation; it is now on the ground – my integrity that I worked so hard to build and maintain for years!" I expected a divine pat on the shoulder and a compassionate endorsement of what I wanted to do to defend myself. This was not forthcoming. Instead I received a divine rebuke: "Jesus made Himself of no reputation." The instruction was to put aside every weapon and ammunition that I had garnered. I was not to defend myself! That was a hard one.

The next few years, obeying God while all types of arrows and darts were flying around me but standing still to see the salvation and deliverance that God Himself would bring was not easy. Ministers of Religion would come up to me and reveal to me the things that they were hearing, being very concerned about my welfare. It was embarrassing, humiliating, heart-rending, to say the least, but I could not defend myself! After one such encounter, when I was presented with a photocopy of my private documents given to a pastor without my knowledge and permission, I was in a Department Store and fainted, crashing into the partial glass covering the items being sold. The edge of the showcase-glass broke and I was slightly injured. All the tests done at the hospital came out negative and it was concluded that my body gave way under tremendous stress. I was put on a week's bed rest with medication. All this time, I continued praying, waiting, walking through forgiveness and wrestling with the Enemy of my soul.

One day, while I was having my devotions, and reading about the Cretans in Titus 1, verses 10 - 12 suddenly jumped out at me. The Holy Spirit instructed me to pray this Scripture at that moment to stop the "mouth" that the Enemy was using against me. I waited for years to be given the strategy and to be released by God to take on the Enemy (Satan who was behind all of this mayhem). When I began to pray that Scripture, the war ceased! God had now released me to pursue, overtake and recover all. Not only did I recover all but like David at Ziklag, I got "double for my trouble" and "brawta" (an overflow). The lesson was clear to me: Sometimes when we are engaged in spiritual war, the victory might not come in the timing that we would want it to. God will allow us to go through the "fire" and He determines when to put out that fire. His promise to us is always sure. When we go through the fire, He will be with us and will not allow it to consume us but will bring us out with not even the smell of fumes on us (Isa. 43:2). Watchmen-intercessors have to learn how to **wait on the Lord** even in the midst of battle.

Fasting Helps Us Win the War

The theme of fasting is attached to this chapter because it was used by Jesus in the context of expelling demons. Jesus said it quite clearly in Matthew 17:21:

"However, this kind does not go out except by prayer and fasting."

(NKJV)

What kind? To what was Jesus referring? The disciples had come to Jesus troubled that they were unable to cast out a particular demon from a lunatic child. The mother, not satisfied to leave her child in this state, went to Jesus and informed Him that she had gone to His disciples and asked them to deliver her child but they were unable to get the job done. After rebuking the disciples' lack of faith, Jesus pointed out that some demonic situations will not move, be broken or be driven out, unless fasting is added to prayer.

FASTING

To **fast** is to abstain for a period of time from some important and necessary activity in our lives in order to accomplish something spiritual. Fasting has a purpose. The believer fasts in order to still the appetites of the body in order to spend focused time with God and to hear from Him without the distractions of the demands of the soul and body. We also see in Matthew 17 mentioned above, that fasting also brings deliverance from demons.

Many of us were taught only the most basic type of fasting: which is abstinence from food or not to place anything in our stomachs (Matt. 4:1, 2). There are however, other types of fasts:

- refraining from sleep (11 Cor. 6:5; 11:27) - e.g. staying up all night to pray

- abstaining from marital sex (1 Cor. 7: 1-5) – with the consent of each partner

- abstaining from anything that takes up much of our time and is enjoyable/pleasurable:

  » watching television

  » reading

  » all types of technological involvement – computers, cell-phones, social media, MP3s, etc.

  » involvement in sports, etc.

I remember doing a test run on this with a gentleman whom I asked the question: *'If you were asked to fast from food or sex for a short period of time, which would you choose?'* Without batting an eyelid, he responded, *'food'*. I thought to myself, it might be more sacrificial for him to fast from sex at times. Fasting is not about what we can easily give up. It is sacrificial in nature. It must cost us something to gain higher heights and deeper depths in God. David knew this principle very well when he retorted to Araunah, "**nor will I offer burnt offerings** to the Lord my God with that which **costs me nothing.**" (2 Samuel 24:24 - NKJV)

The National Intercessory Prayer Network of Jamaica (NIPNOJ) has an annual 21-day fast usually beginning the second Sunday in September. A few years ago, while on one of these fasts (abstaining from food), the Holy Spirit clearly instructed me to fast from television. I thought that this would be so easy until...! I had such a battle, not with the food but with the tube. I did not realize that I had somewhat of an addiction. I truly needed fasting to break this craving for television-watching. After that fast, and receiving deliverance, I decided to gauge my television watching. This also went for anything else I found pleasurable and entertaining. I had to admit to myself that I loved to be entertained. I therefore set up alert buttons in my brain so that nothing would "control me". 1 Cor. 6:12 states:

> *"All things are lawful unto me, but all things are not expedient: all things are lawful for me, but I will not be brought under the power of any."*

> *(KJV)*

The writing of this book coincided with the annual fast for this year. About the second week of the fast, my husband and I independently received from the Lord that we should extend the 21 days to 40 days. We shared it with our intercessors and they joined us. Another prayer general in our nation had also received the same instructions for her people who were about to begin a 21- day fast. It was not difficult for us to respond to God although many bodies were under attack.

While the fast was going on, approximately 70 percent of Jamaicans were struck by the Chikungunya virus (chikv) that hit the nation like a plague. This virus was transmitted by a special breed of mosquitoes. It touched anyone, at any level or strata in the society. Sometimes entire households were struck, experiencing high fever, joint pains, rashes, headaches, nausea, fainting spells and no one could help the other. Several deaths occurred among those who were vulnerable with pre-existing medical conditions such as diabetes, heart issues, high blood pressure, etc. Some of the elderly were not strong enough to survive. The nation needed this type of intense prayer and fasting at that time in order to survive and rebound from this horrible epidemic. During the fast, God laid on my heart to pray from 1 Kings 8:37-39. Wherever I went to pray concerning this and the threat of Ebola, another scare which was looming globally, I prayed from the Word of God – if there be any sickness, any plague, any disease, Oh Lord hear… forgive and ACT!

NIPNOJ's Intercessors' Camp took place during the period of this fast – coincidentally or one might say it was God-incidentally - as it was postponed from its usual time in July. A second postponement seemed inevitable as many of the intercessors were going under with chikv. The Lord instructed us however, that we were "going over" and not "under" with this camp. The Camp was held with adults and children (including a 5 month old baby, Joshua Smith) who went into the hills and fasted and prayed from Thursday to Sunday. God preserved our health and our strength. It was one of the best camps NIPNOJ has had since the first one held in 1995. All praise to our God for those who received deliverance from tormenting spirits at the camp; breakthroughs with stubborn situations and those who came into freedom to go on to the next level in their walk with God. This I believe, especially with the national crisis, happened successfully because God's intercessors were obedient and came apart to pray and to fast before Him.

Many biblical characters practiced fasting when they needed uncommon breakthroughs, personally or within their nations:

- Nehemiah –fasted when he heard of the devastating state of his nation. He found favour and got leave from the king to rebuild the walls of Jerusalem. (Neh.1:4)

- Daniel - fasted for 21 days regarding his people and although there was spiritual warfare in the heavenlies in an attempt to hinder the angel bringing the answer to him, the angel over-came. (Dan. 10:2-3)

- Esther - called for a 3-day fast for all the Jews in her city to destroy the plans of a wicked man, Haman, who was bent on destroying her people, the Jews. The situation turned around and the major intercessor in that account was promoted to national leadership. (Esther 4:15-17)

- Moses - fasted for 40 days on more than one occasion out of which he received the 10 commandments on which many other laws were built even to this day.

- Paul - God called him and healed him from blindness during a fast. (Acts 9:9-12)

- Jesus – fasted for 40 days and was empowered by the Holy Spirit to begin his earthly ministry. (Luke 4:1-14)

Interestingly enough, even before Jesus came to earth, men were fasting and knew the secret power behind denying oneself in order to get the full attention of the God of the universe. Other religions have practiced fasting too but for the Christian, there is only one God to whom we have dedicated our lives and we know beyond a shadow of a doubt, that our sacrifices in fasting will never go in vain unless we refuse to fast the way He has taught us to in Isaiah 58. The watchman-intercessor has to watch his life and his walk so that his fasting will bear much fruit. He therefore has to ensure, according to this passage, that he meets God's requirements for fasting and therefore share in God's benefits to those who make this sacrifice before Him.

REQUIREMENTS FOR FASTING

- *Setting Captives Free* -- To loose the bands of wickedness, to undo the heavy burdens, and to let the oppressed go free, and that you break every yoke (Isa 58:6 - KJV)

- *Reaching out to the Poor and Needy* -- Is it not to share your bread with the hungry, And that you bring to your house the poor who are cast out; When you see the naked, that you cover him, And not hide yourself from your own flesh?? (Isa 58:7 - NKJV)

- *Stemming Self-centred Practices* -- If thou take away from the midst of thee the yoke, the putting forth of the finger, and speaking vanity;. (Isa 58:9 - KJV)

- *Extending Compassion and Grace* -- And if thou draw out thy soul to the hungry, and satisfy the afflicted soul;... (Isa 58:10 - KJV)

- *Respecting the Day Dedicated to God* -- If you turn away your foot from the Sabbath, from doing your pleasure on My holy day... (Isa 58:13 - NKJV)

BENEFITS OF FASTING

- Then shall *your light break forth* as the morning, and

- Your *health shall spring forth speedily*: and

- Your righteousness shall go before you;

- The glory of the LORD shall be your rereward. (Isa 58:8)

- Then shalt *you call, and the LORD shall answer; you shall cry,* and *he shall say, Here I am.* (Isa 58:9)

- Then shall *your light rise in obscurity* and your darkness *be* as the noonday. (Isa 58:10)

- And the *LORD shall guide you* continually, and *satisfy your soul* in drought, and make fat your bones: and you shall be like a watered garden, and like a spring of water, whose waters fail not. (Isa 58:11)

- And *they that shall be* of you shall build the old waste places: you shall raise up the foundations of many generations; and you shall be called, *The repairer* of the breach, *The restorer* of paths to dwell in. (Isa 58:12) Then shall you delight yourself in the LORD; and I will cause you to ride upon the high places of the earth, and feed you with the heritage of Jacob your father. (Isa 58:14)

(King James Version)

My Own Conquests Through Fasting

From the early stages of Christianity, in particular my early years in seminary, I began to learn through experience, the wisdom and potency of adding fasting to my prayer. I was faced with an onslaught of temptations that would have, if I had given in, weakened my faith and devastated my testimony, at least for me, even if no one found out. I cried out to God constantly in prayer to help me not to fall but I felt myself weakening more and more. I truly got scared. The one thing I did not want to be was a double-standard Christian!

The Holy Spirit led me to fast for one week. I obeyed. At the end of that week, I not only felt the return of my strength but I was able to confront the situation. I also got the boldness to challenge and rebuke the person who the Enemy was using to lure me into situations. After that confrontation, the individual never approached me again and actually walked far from me. I still give God thanks for that deliverance and how He responded to my fasting and prayer.

Another occasion came later while I was still in seminary. I began dating someone who was much older than I. I began to feel uncomfortable about the relationship and more importantly about his real stance with the Lord, although he was a religious and decent person. I began to have doubts. An older female friend encouraged me however, pointing out how well he would take care of me. He was very kind and gentle, gave great gifts, already owned his own home and vehicle, but the discomfort grew. I decided to do what worked before. Fasting.

I fasted about the situation and God gave me the peace to break off the relationship. I was a bit intimidated in the relationship as this person was older but after the fast I gained the fortitude to gently but firmly explain that the relationship had to end. Surprisingly, although obviously disappointed, he released me peacefully and we could be cordial with each other the few times we met afterwards. Years after, I could congratulate him when we met on a school compound where he had come to pick up his daughter, the first child from his marriage. Although I was still single, I had no regrets for obeying God and was still grateful to God for helping me through fasting to make that life-changing decision.

As the years went by and my responsibilities increased to include planning national events like NIPNOJ's Annual Intercessors' Camp (we just completed the 20th) and international events to which other nations were invited (The Caribbean Prayer Summit), I know that these events would either have not come off or there would have been serious casualties if my planning committees and I did not know how critical fasting was in breaking yokes in order to bring forth the will of God. The Caribbean Prayer Summits which were held in Barbados, Suriname and Jamaica each had its own set of demonic forces to overcome. The territorial spirits assaulted us while planning and executing each summit. We could not anticipate the level and nature of spiritual warfare that each nation would present. At the end of these events, we believed our lives and the lives, health, finances and ministries of our loved ones, ministry partners and attendees were spared because God had taught us the dynamics of prayer coupled with fasting in spiritual warfare.

There is no major event that we undertake as a ministry that is not undergirded by fasting, even if it is the leaders alone who fast. Our experiences and those of others have indelibly highlighted in our minds the critical need to practice this discipline of the Christian life. If Jesus had to fast; what say you and I? Many battles are fought on our knees and won when we put aside the appetites, so God we can please.

CHAPTER **6**

Interceding for the Family

Nothing tends more to cement the hearts of Christians than praying together. Never do they love one another so well as when they witness the outpouring of each other's hearts in prayer.

Charles Finney

INTERCEDING FOR THE family, though a natural inclination of the heart to cry out to God for those we love, can be one of the most difficult things to do. Some intercessors have found themselves erring in praying for others while ignoring their own family members. Others have blundered on the other side of the pendulum, in always praying for their loved ones but ignoring the rest of the world. God's desire is for intercessors to stand in-the-gap for their own family members as well as for concerns outside of the family. Why would Christians generally and watchmen-intercessors specifically find it an irksome task to pray for their own families?

One reason for this is that the family is the place that can **make** you or **break** you. It is such a dynamic institution that research has proven that this was the place, especially in our formative years that set much of our foundation for life. Some stalwarts in the faith and in our nations were made because of proper ground work done in the family. On the other hand, many criminal elements that haunt our societies have been who they are with the influence of dysfunctional families, especially those who were exposed to the occult. Some have had to spend much resources and uncountable times in the prayer closet cleaning up the chaos in their lives which they inherited from their families of origin / consecutive households that they lived in. It is the power of the Gospel of Christ that has saved many individuals from continuing in abnormal and ungodly behaviours passed down within the family line through generational curses and improper models.

A second reason is that since family relationships are ongoing, there can be times of serious discouragement especially when we are not seeing any obvious manifestations of change (answer to our prayers). Having to live with certain conditions facing the family on a day-to-day basis and not seeing any obvious breakthroughs can be disheartening. Some have lost faith in God, their belief in the power of prayer and many have simply walked away from trying to fix things in the family.

Another reason why prayer is weak within families is that our family members are usually the ones who "know us after the flesh" especially our weakness and can be the blindest ones to who we are / have become through the power of God at work in lives. Jesus was a great example of this misunderstanding. In Luke 4:24, Jesus put it this way, "No prophet is accepted in his own country." (cf. John 4:24 - KJV). It was Jesus' family who came to pull him away from ministering (Mark 3:31). His comment on who is His mother, sister and brother, could suggest that they did not understand that He had to do what He was doing, which is the will of His Father (Matt. 12:48-50). The family can also be a place of most intense negative feelings of anger, resentment and unforgiveness in husband-wife, parent-child and sibling relationships. In societies where many generations live in the same home or extended family members, this conflict expands. This is not a modern-day phenomenon. Matt. 10: 36 informs us that "A man's foes will be they of his own household." (KJV) (Micah 7:6). The Scriptures address some of these relational issues within the family.

- **Husband and wife**: 1 Peter 3:7 - Likewise ye husbands, dwell with them according to knowledge ...and as being heirs to-gether of the grace of life; that your prayers be not hindered (KJV). (Otherwise you cannot pray effectively – Amplified Bible)

- **Parent – child**: Ephesians 6:1- 4 - Children obey ...honour your parents ...that all may be well ....you may live long ....Fathers, do not provoke your children ....

- **Sibling Relationships:** Genesis 4:3-8 - (Story of Cain and Abel); Esau and Jacob (Genesis 25-27); Joseph and his broth-ers (Genesis 37 – 50)

Looking at the possible family dynamics from the Scriptures and examining the modern-day family, it is for these reasons and more that we need to pray for our family members. The watchman-intercessor needs to be watching over his/her own family in the following areas. Primarily, intercession should be made for their salvation, regardless of their deportment. God should be petitioned for the welfare of each member, not giving up on any. Each relationship should be covered by prayer knowing that Satan goes about like a roaring lion seeking who he may devour and many times going after the strongest (the leader) and the weakest (the children) (1 Peter 5:8).

Some general reasons why intercession is necessary for the

family begins with the fact that the Scripture indicates that our entire households can be saved (Acts 10:24, 44; 16:31). God's desire and will is that none should perish (Ezek. 18:23). Whether we like it or not, the love of Christ shown to us in our salvation, impels us to (II Cor. 5:14). It is interesting that the Scripture also states it as a requirement for God to acknowledge and respond to our fasting and prayer (Isa. 58:6-7). Our spirituality is not counted if we ignore our own flesh and blood. Then there is the compassionate-obligatory reason. Many are saved today because someone prayed generally or specifically and took the time to share the Gospel. It would therefore be a selfish act not to desire to see those of our households saved.

How to Pray for Our Loved Ones

The following guidelines were found on a strip of paper, without a name attached, but was wisely penned and deemed by this author as worthy of sharing.

- Find out God's will and purpose for their lives. (Rom. 8:26)

- Establish a FAMILY ALTAR. (Gen. 48:13-20)

- Operate with them in LOVE. (Prov. 10:12; I Cor. 13)

  » In order for us to love this way we have to learn to deal with offences before they become WALLS in our relationships!

- Go after their "FELT NEEDS". (II Kings 5:1-14

- Felt Needs of Each Member:-

  » Husbands – respect, appreciation, marital needs fulfilled, etc. (I Cor. 7:3-5, 17; I Pet. 3:1-5)

» Wives – love and affection, consideration, etc. (Eph. 5:28-33; I Pet. 3:7)

» Children – love, encouragement, acceptance. (Eph. 6:4) (I would add TIME spent with them which for a child spells LOVE!)

In order to pray effectively for the family, there are some *hindrances* that need to be removed. Resentment, anger, unforgiveness are three of the biggest hindrances and Ps. 66:18 already warns us that if iniquity is in our hearts, "the Lord will not hear" (NAS). The dishonouring of parents, even by adult children and the dishonouring of a spouse are other hindrances (Eph. 6:1-4; I Pet. 6:7). It is obvious that God expects in our family relationships, for us to show respect for each other, regardless of the circumstances. There is no qualification given for the type of parents or spouses that one should honour. Envy, jealousy, strife, selfishness creates a stomping ground in the family for the Enemy. He operates in a rampant fashion when these are present. It is no wonder that the individuals would find it difficult to pray, especially together (James 4:1-10).

Another often overlooked hindrance is discouragement which usually comes where there is disappointment – nothing seems to change. II Cor. 4:1 however exhorts us not to lose heart / faint in our faith.

The personal intercessory life of the watchman-intercessor is what was specifically addressed above. There is however, another aspect that needs to be addressed and the watchman-intercessor could take leadership in this aspect, being sensitive to the Holy Spirit. This is the setting up of a **Family Altar**, where God can be met, as many times as possible, by the entire family. This should ideally be set up and led by the head of the household, however, if the leader is not a Christian or is inactive as a Christian, he/she should be consulted and the idea shared first with them. This is adopting God's order in the family. If the watchman-intercessor is the leader in the home then it is his duty to initiate this altar.

The Family Altar is a time set apart within the family for corporate Bible study, worship and prayer. This is an opportunity for each family member to pray; for individual family members to be prayed for regarding felt needs; for struggles, even among family members to be shared for the purpose of God's intervention and for the general needs of the family to be presented to God by this unit. It is one way of affirming and confirming that God is at the centre of a home and fulfilling the declaration, as Joshua did, that "as for me and my house, we will serve the Lord." (Joshua 24:15- NASB).

As a family, with the fast-paced lifestyle of both parents working and getting our son off to school on time, we have had to take our family altar to the car. It is as we spend time in traffic that our time is used in prayer and in worship. After a breakfast meal, the Scripture and a devotional reading is done. We have found that the time spent on the road is such precious quantity of time that we are unable to recoup when we are at home, especially for focused quality praying together. The car becomes that "closet" where, as a unit, we can shut out the world and speak to our Father in heaven. For prayer as a couple, my husband and I have had to find ways and means to ensure that we are able to have our personal requests aired in prayer, together. One innovative way we have adopted is on our walks together for the purpose of exercising. Though the prayers are shorter then, we are able to address and make declarations over circumstances that we are faced with.

If the Family Altar is broken down in the watchman-intercessors family, it can be repaired (1 Kings 18:30). How do you prepare this altar? By recognizing that it is broken down; confessing that it should have been erected and being serviced; invite family members to participate in this time of devotion to God, explaining the benefits of having such an Altar and being persistent in maintaining this Altar, as many things will assail the family, even to specifically, destroy this Altar. Satan hates the agreement and unity in prayer that could be experienced during these times and more so, the answers to prayer that could come to strengthen the faith of family members.

INTERCESSION THAT WORKED FOR A FAMILY

There is a family, one of many, where I have seen intercession work. The daughter, who we will call Tamara (name changed for privacy), was obviously under oppression by the Enemy, Satan and his cohorts. There were cuttings, suicidal attempts, rebellion, tantrums, a resistance to the things of God, and the list goes on. Tamara's mother and a group of intercessors relentlessly stood in intercession for that teen. The more we prayed, the worse things seem to become. We had to keep our eyes fixed on Jesus. We began to declare to the Enemy of her soul, "Not this one... not now and not ever!" We stood our ground and declared God's promises given to the "seed of the righteous" (Psalm 112:1-2).

It seemed like suddenly the miracle began to happen. Tamara made a turn. She began to go to Church without being told. Her grades rose in school where she became an honour student, a student leader and later a scholarship recipient. She upon entering college was elected student leader from the beginning. It was not easy to keep up the fight against the forces of darkness that assailed her life. We knew one mother who was relentless in the war and ensured that others would not forget to pray for her precious daughter. She and that family have received "double for their trouble". She has made that family proud as they can now all serve God together.

The watchman-intercessor must receive God's encouragement today and be emboldened to pray for family members / to set up a Family Altar. It is imperative that their hearts be emptied of all offences and malice so that they can truly stand before God and sincerely intercede on behalf of individual family members and for them to be heard when inviting family members to the Family Altar. This indeed will be pleasing to God

CHAPTER 7

Interceding for the Church

When a Christian shuns fellowship with other Christians, the Devil smiles. When he stops studying the Bible, the Devil laughs. When he stops praying the Devil shouts for joy.

Corrie Ten Boom

ONE MAY THINK, why intercede for the Church, shouldn't the Church be interceding for others. In the same way that one might ask, why intercede for a Prayer Ministry or for intercessors? The fact is that everyone needs prayers. Every institution needs prayers. Since prayer is getting God's Kingdom to come on earth, knowing the mind of God and to ensure that His will supersedes all others (Luke 11:2), then every sphere of life needs to be touched by prayer, including the Church. As a matter of fact, if the Church, individual fellowships, is not supported by prayer, much of God's Will will not be done since the Church is God's hands and feet to advance His Will in the earth.

The first group of persons who need prayer within the Church fellowships are its leaders. Every pastor should have a band of intercessors bringing him/her before the throne of God on a daily basis. They need to be covered in prayer for every aspect of their ministry – preparing sermons, visitations and caring for the sheep, their marriage and family life, their health and finances and their relationships with others. As much as the pastor is sought out to pray for others, even more so, many prayers should be made on his/her behalf. The truth is that the best way to scatter sheep, members of a fellowship, is to strike the shepherd, the one who is primarily leading that flock.

Jesus' Example

It is interesting to note that while Jesus was on earth, he interceded for the Church (John 17). The outline of His prayer could give us some guidelines.

- Jesus prayed setting out the facts - the Body of Christ receives eternal life only through Jesus (vs 2 - 3); He had completed His purpose on earth which was to glorify the Father and manifest Him to others, an instructive clause for believers in our own mandates today (vs 4, 6, 26).

- The Church as Focus - there comes a time in our prayer when the people of God must be the focal point of our praying, not the world, in spite of the fact that intercessors do pray for the world (v 9).

- The Church's Battle in the World - the Church needs to be prayed for because Christians are still "in the world" and have to contend with that world (v 11).

- The importance of Jesus' joy being in the believer's life - it was Jesus' desire for His joy to be made full, complete and perfect in the life of each believer (v 13).

- The Church is an object of hate - prayer is needed for the believers because they have become enemies of the world – now hated by the world (v 14).

- The Church is targeted by Satan - Prayer is needed to cover and protect God's people from the evil one (v 15).

- Prayers for the sanctification of the Church through the truth of God's Word (vs 17 – 19).

- Prayer is to be made for those who will become a part of Jesus' Church through the preaching of the Gospel (v 20).

- Unity...unity...unity! A critical part of the Lord praying on this occasion. This unity was for the purpose of properly convincing the world about Who Jesus is and His love for them with the end result being faith in Him, arising in the unbeliever's life (vs 21-23).

- Jesus has had it seems, an intense desire for His people to be with Him, not only to know that the Church belonged to Him but that His people will be where He is (v 24).

THE APOSTLE PAUL'S EXHORTATIONS

We are exhorted in the Scriptures, especially by Paul's special requests for prayer. As the man who is credited as the author of 13 of the 27 books in the New Testament; an intellectual; one who laid the foundation of much of Christian theology; he still needed prayer! He needed prayer for he always recognized that he was also human and had weaknesses (2 Cor. 12:7-10). With this consciousness in spite of the fact that he was a stalwart leader, a great Apostle of the faith, one who had mighty visitations from God, he begged for prayer: Romans 15:30 - "I appeal to you [I entreat you], brethren, for the sake of our

Lord Jesus Christ and by the love [given by] the Spirit, to unite with me in earnest wrestling in prayer to God in my behalf." (AMP) 1 Thess. 5: 25 - Brethren, pray for us. The prayers of the saints was key to his deliverance from death (2 Cor. 1:9 – 11); to circumstances turning around in his favour (Phill. 1:19) and that through their prayers a way would be open for him (Philemon 1:22).

Peter Wagner, a prayer general, pointed out in his book, *Prayer Shield*, that 5% of church members in the average church provide 80% of the meaningful intercession (p. 40). Even without this research being done, one could have easily made this approximation by looking at the size of a Church's membership and the quantity that turns out to its prayer meetings. Compare and contrast this to the attendance especially for social gatherings within the same fellowship. This trend should be a primary focus for prayer. Jesus, in a moment of intense passion and zeal for His Church exclaimed that it is written that, "My house shall be called a house of ***prayer.***" (Matt. 21:13-KJV). The majority of Church fellowships are known on the streets not for prayer but for great praise and worship; grand programmes; fun social activities; impacting social programmes; warm care cell meetings and the list goes on. These aspects of a fellowship are important but there is a problem if rarely does anyone say, whether within the walls of a Church or beyond, this is truly a house of prayer!

The questions that need to be asked within the Church are: Is prayer no longer attractive, personally and corporately? Do we have to turn to focus on all types of gimmicks at the risk of the death of prayer, in order to attract the masses? Did Jesus resort to any special effects and tactics to draw persons to His Father? Or did He not say, "If I be lifted up" (always made the centre), I "will draw all *peoples* to Myself." (John 12:32 - NKJV)? May Jesus help every Church leader, board, members and intercessors, to wrestle in prayer until prayer becomes a reality and the hallmark of the Church as Jesus intended it to be.

Pastors / Church Leaders Urgently Need Intercession

Pastors pray for people. This is one of the things they are expected to do. But who really prays for the pastor – discerningly, wisely, with knowledge and understanding. It is known that church governments do not lay out their personal issues before the congregation. The congregation could not carry those burdens as they are usually in need of leaders assisting them in carrying theirs. To whom does the pastor go for strong spiritual support; when they are faced with overwhelming temptations? For many, it is only their spouse, who also can carry so much and no more along with generally supporting him/her in ministry and taking care of much of the family needs in order to facilitate this ministry. The fact is that there is a *cost* to being a pastor/church leader. Peter Wagner points out what some of these costs are:

- They have to constantly present an ***image to the public.*** Many of them are put on a pedestal. Where/to whom do they go for help?

- Many are ***vulnerable to the attacks of the Enemy***. The main downfall of pastors/leaders now is burnout and sexual immorality. 20% of pastors in U.S.A. fall into the sin of sexual immorality.

- They have more responsibility and accountability. They are judged more for who they are and not what they do (James 3:1).

- Leaders are more subject to temptation. Greed, power and pride are temptations.

> *Make no mistake about it, the higher up you go on the ladder of Christian leadership, the higher you go on Satan's hit list. (Wagner, "Prayer Shield", p.67)*

> *Money and power team up with sex as some of the strongest lures for ministers. (Ibid)*

- They are subject to direct demonic attacks through demonization, spells, curses and incantations (1 Peter 5:8).

- Pastors/church leaders are more targeted by spiritual warfare. Satanists, witches, New Agers, occultists.

- Pastors have more influence on others - the fall of a pastor injures more people and affects the church.

- Pastors have more visibility - they are constantly subject to gossip and criticism. (Wagner, page 67 - 70)

Much of Wagner's surveys were done prior to 1994, prior to the publishing of the first edition of his book. This was when the internet was not being accessed by many; pornography was not as accessible as it is now on cable, cell phones, tablets and computers. "Sexting" (texting sexually explicit contents) was perhaps not thought possible and generally the culture of sin and perversion was not as openly crusaded and celebrated. Church leaders being human are subject to the same temptations as the regular congregant is and more so.

Wagner also shares about two surveys which are very relevant to our topic of the urgent need for praying for pastors and other church leaders. Wagner's Survey of 572 pastors revealed that the average time pastors spent in prayer daily was 22 minutes. 28% or 1 out of 4 prayed less than 10 minutes a day!

Another survey, showed, however that intercession improved their ministry (especially when it was done daily) and it seemed to help Church growth. If one is honestly looking at the demands of the pastoral role, one would have to ask, when would the pastor be able to have quality time in the presence of the Lord on a personal basis? Wouldn't there be struggles to have a balanced devotional life with the daily pressures, deadlines, phone calls (early morning too) and "emergencies" (having to put out many "fires" in marriages and families; sometimes in the community). Who really stops to ask about their spiritual life and how they might be coping with all of the burdens placed on them? Isn't it normally assumed that they are doing well?

Without knowing much about the personal life of an individual pastor/church leader, the watchman-intercessor should ask God to give him/her an understanding of what it is like to lead a Church and to ask for specific instructions from God regarding the issues he/she should pray for Church leadership in general but specifically his/her own Church leaders. Intercessors should also be trained in this role since it is critical for a Church leader to stand at the front of the army, leading with strength, without being struck down. May God raise up many who will stand-in-the-gap in their fellowships and ensure that the "gates of hell" will not prevail against it (Matt. 16:18).

CHAPTER 8

Interceding for the Nation

The third petition of the Lord's Prayer is repeated daily by millions who have not the slightest intention of letting anyone's will be done but their own.

Aldous Huxley

I BECAME A Christian in the late 1970s, the era of the Charismatic Movement and would accredit much of my burden of interceding for my nation to the vision and passion of some of the leaders of this movement. There was one leader who was dubbed "the nation man" because of his passionate plea to us to pray for the Government, Opposition, issues involving the poor, justice and righteousness. Since that time, before even knowing what intercession was all about, God placed a similar burden in my heart for my nation. This burden led me to represent Jamaica at many international intercessory conventions and summits. The first of these being in Israel in 1994 and later in 1996 at the All Nations Convocation hosted by Jerusalem House of Prayer For All Nations.

But it was not only about representing my nation at these international events; it was also about traveling all over Jamaica stirring the people of God to focus on the nation. At many of the national events where I had to stand-in-the-gap on public platforms, there was such an overwhelming burden of Identificational Repentance. Every sin of the nation was at that moment, as if it were my own sin. This also happened in Israel as the Ethiopians approached me on both occasions to inform me that my nation was resented in some way by them because of those who had come under the rule of Emperor Haile Selassie and had destroyed areas of their country. It was not easy to have to stand on the platform of an event with representatives from 180 countries, listening to another nation requesting forgiveness for how they viewed Jamaicans and I having to ask their forgiveness on behalf of my people. This request for forgiveness was not only followed by intercession on Mount Zion, for these atrocities but also declarations of the promises of God for my country which was to be a blessing in the earth! The forgiveness that flowed and the reconciliation that followed can hardly be expressed in words. This was a "God moment" at these conventions when God intervened in the affairs of nations and brought reconciliation, some of these we saw evidence of the answers to prayers prayed in Israel, in the international media as nations who were at odds began to take steps, in the natural, to reconcile.

Repentance Needed In Every Nation

Every nation knowingly or obliviously sins against God from its leadership to the ordinary man in its streets. This sin sometimes takes the form of evil and wickedness done within that nation among its people or atrocities committed against other nations, both of which need divine forgiveness.

Isaiah 1 and Ezekiel 8 paint the picture of a nation that God was displeased with. Let us remember that this nation was also the people of God. What were some things that went wrong?

- *"there is* no soundness in it; *but* wounds, and bruises, and putrefying (rotting) sores" (Isa 1:6). This nation was a wounded nation with a broken people who needed God's healing touch.

- "strangers devour it in your presence, and *it is* desolate…" This nation was overtaken by foreign forces and every area was impacted by strangers taking over. This nation had lost its ability to sovereignly rule itself.

- "Bring no more vain oblations; incense is an abomination unto me" God was weary of their religious practices, leaders and followers who were not living in obedience to His laws. God's description of the religious things was, *"it is* iniquity" – they were displeasing to Him.

- There was Bloodguiltiness which will be discussed in more details as a scourge within a nation. "When ye make many prayers, I will not hear: **your hands are full of blood**. (v. 15)

- Ezekiel 8 highlights the issue of idolatry, another blight on the record of any nation. The consequences of idolatry were severe. God's wrath was poured out on every sector of society beginning with the leaders in the sanctuary. (Ezekiel 9:6-10)

(King James Version)

THE FOURFOLD REMEDY

Isaiah 1:16- 19:

1. Confess and Repent – "Wash you, make you clean…" (v 16)

2. Stop and Turn – turn from your wicked ways – "cease to do evil" (v 16)

3. Employ Loving Actions – learn to walk righteously - "seek judgment, relieve the oppressed, judge the fatherless, plead for the widow". (v 17)

4. Start An Obedient Walk With God – Come to God – "Come now, and let us reason together... If ye be willing and obedient, ye shall eat the good of the land." (v 18-19)

(King James Version)

Repent... Turn... Love God and man!

God seems to have a divine predisposition towards the poor and oppressed, the fatherless and the widows. When we fail to attend to these persons and worse, when we cause them to get angry and they have to cry to God for help, that nation is in trouble!

There are consequences if we choose to / not to apply this fourfold remedy:

- Individuals and the land will prosper - if we obey God by repenting and returning to Him. (Isa 1:19) - If we are willing and obedient, we shall eat the good of the land.

- A *refusal* to do this will lead to that nation's demise - (Isa 1:20) - if we refuse and rebel, we shall be devoured with the sword (gun / any other weapon).

There is a question God asks and so should we if we are living in a backslidden nation - How is the faithful city become an harlot! It was full of judgment; righteousness lodged in it; **but now murderers**. (Isa 1:21)

The Shedding of Innocent Blood

Deuteronomy 21:1-9 is one of the passages in Scriptures which shows us the severity of shedding innocent blood, whether or not it was intentional. It is usually referred to as **Bloodguiltiness** since the entire principality is held accountable and therefore guilty, whether all the citizens are aware of the bloodshed or not. (Deut. 21: 1; 19:10; Jer. 26:15) Those who are leaders in that principality, the elders and judges had to act before God to do something about the guilt. (v 2-3) That bloodguilt needed **atonement**; therefore sacrifice had to be made with atoning blood. (v 4) The priests who were also intercessors had to come to God because He would hear THEM! (v 5)

How do we know this as a fact? The Scripture says, "by their word shall every controversy and every assault shall be settled" (v. 5 - NKJV). This is not strange since God had already had a similar response when Moses came in-the-gap in repentance on behalf of Israel. God said to Moses: "I have pardoned according to YOUR word." (Numb.14:20 - KJV). God pardoned the nation of Israel because like a skilled advocate and mediator, Moses stood before the Righteous Judge of the universe and pleaded for Israel.

There were however some cautions and precautions: None of them standing there should be either guilty of the act OR have knowledge of the one who is guilty but is withholding it. (v 6-7)

When intercession was made, the guilt of blood was forgiven and land purged. (v 8 - 9)

SOME PRINCIPLES ABOUT SHEDDING INNOCENT BLOOD

- When innocent blood is shed, it has to be *atoned for*. This is God's requirement (Deut. 21:8 - 9)

- An entire household + generation can *bear that guilt* until it is dealt with. (I Kings 2:31)

- It is seen as *evil* in the eyes of the Lord. (II Kings 21:16)

- *Forgiveness* has to be sought. (II Kings 24:4f)

- Innocent blood shed *desecrates* (damages, vandalizes, defiles, violates, insults, pollutes) the land (Ps. 106:38)

- God *hates* (detests, is disgusted, abhors, loathes, can't stand or bear, is repulsed by) hands that shed innocent blood (Prov. 6:17)

- A land that sheds innocent blood, that country can, because of God's judgement, become *desolate* (barren, depressing, gloomy, unwelcoming) and a desert waste.(Joel 3:19)

- Only *God* can deliver a person/city/nation from bloodguiltiness. (Psalm 51:14)

- Demons want blood sacrifice too. (Ps. 106: 37- 38 - ...sons and daughters sacrificed to idols of Canaan.)

- Even a king / ruler is judged by God for shedding innocent blood. (Jer. 22:15 – 19) – Jehoiakim, king of Judah was "buried with the burial of a donkey" being dragged out of the city).

So Ezekiel was asked, in another passage which addresses Bloodguiltiness, Ezekiel 22:1-5, "will you judge the bloody city? Yes, show her all her abominations!" (v 2 - NKJV) The man of God was expected to show that city its abominable ways. It was as if God expected him to and he could not be silent. Judgement was coming anyway on that city (v 3). Guilt was pronounced upon that city. "You have become guilty by the blood which you have shed" (v 4 - NKJV). The word **guilty** means to be held in, bound by, liable to a charge or action at law; responsibility for criminal or moral offence. (Collins Shorter Dictionary and Thesaurus)

As a result, that city was made a **reproach** - "...therefore have I made you a **reproach** (v 4 - AMP) This means it became something disgraceful and discredited; an object of abuse by words spoken against it. Sometimes it is defeat in battle because of enmity. Jer. 24:9:

> I will deliver them to trouble into all the kingdoms of the earth, for their harm, to be a reproach and a byword, a taunt and a curse, in all places where I shall drive them. (NKJV)

It is not a new phenomenon that money was often paid to destroy the innocent. Prov. 29:10 . The bloodthirsty hate the blameless man. This was even true in the New Testament as money was paid to Jesus' betrayer. Matt 27:6 - "... for it is the price of blood." (KJV)

The opposite of guilt is **guiltless** - naqah (Hebrew) - to be pure, innocent, being 'free' from wrongdoing and punishment (Numb 5:31; Exod. 21:19); to be acquitted, cleansed, held innocent; to be released. Which nation would not want to stand before God guiltless? Maybe every nation. However, being guiltless before God comes with conditions. No nation / city is left in the dark concerning these conditions. The Scriptures have laid them out clearly and a nation can prosper if it chooses to heed these conditions. From the passages explored, it is evident that the watchmen-intercessors within a nation have to position themselves to deal with the issues that are an abomination to God. The welfare of that nation is laid squarely in the hands of the Body of Christ. If the intercessors don't move to pray, especially that God's people will meet his requirements for the welfare of the nation, the results will be hazardous, not for the secular aspects of that nation alone but definitely for the Church.

> If my people, which are called by my name, shall humble themselves, and pray, and seek my face, and turn from their wicked ways; then will I hear from heaven, and will forgive their sin, and will heal their land.

> *(2Chronicles 7:14- KJV)*

2 Samuel 21 is another passage of Scripture which addresses the matter of the shedding of innocent blood and its consequences upon a nation. A three-year famine struck the nation of Israel under King David's rule. Being a righteous ruler and a man after God's own heart, he inquired of the Lord. Seems like God was waiting on this inquiry and answered him. "And the LORD said, "*It is* because of Saul and *his* bloodthirsty house, because he killed the Gibeonites. (2Sa 21:1- NKJV) The Gibeonites were those who deceived Joshua decades before and Joshua had made a vow to them that they would not be killed. (Joshua 9:15) King David summoned the Gibeonites and his question to them is rather instructive: "with what shall I make atonement, that you may bless the inheritance of the Lord?"(v3 - NKJV)

Firstly, there was seen by the king, the need to atone for Bloodguiltiness. He took responsibility for whatever atrocity they had encountered by Israel. Secondly, he recognized that that had left a curse upon his nation resulting in God allowing food shortage and deprivation in the land. This curse he acknowledged by his request, could only be removed by the offended party lifting it and bestowing on Israel their blessing. The result was a bloody encounter. It takes the shedding of blood to atone for the sin of murder! Thanks be to God that Jesus' blood became that atoning blood so that now intercessors can call on God to atone for Bloodguiltiness through the efficacious blood of Jesus. Thirdly, the request was granted on their terms. David handed over seven sons of Saul to be killed to bring about this atonement. The results: the famine broke. (v 14) "….after that God heeded the prayer for the land." (NKJV)

HOW TO INTERCEDE FOR A NATION

The Scriptures have given us guidelines to assist us to do the inevitable, interceding for our nation which is going to fall short of God's glory. Here are some recommendations:

- Start at the beginning which is where the Scripture exhorts us to start.

I exhort therefore, that, first of all, supplications, prayers, inter-cessions, and giving of thanks, be made for all men; For kings, and for all that are in authority; that we may lead a quiet and peaceable life in all godliness and honesty.

(1 Timothy 2:1–2-KJV)

There are Christians, including intercessors, who struggle with this passage which tells us that we should place priority on praying for our Government (kings and all that are in authority). The struggle many times comes from disappointment in particular leaders, hurtful encounters that that nation has with its leadership and sometimes it is straight bias. We enter party politics into play with what God desires, so if the party one chooses is not the party in leadership, one's prayer weakens or does not happen on behalf of those in office at all.

The Scriptures and modern day history have exposed us to some wicked leaders. I believe however, that if Christians were not interceding for God to change the heart of the king or to intervene in any way He chooses to stop them, then the turn for the better of the nations under their rule would not have happened. Proverbs 21:1 tells us exactly who is in control. "The king's heart is in the hand of the LORD, as the rivers of water: he turns it wherever he wishes. (NKJV)." What a comfort this is to those who depend on God to lead their nations into the right path. Can you imagine if this were not possible?

There is a good reason given in 1 Timothy 2:1-2, however, why it is necessary to pray for the nation – *"that we may lead a quiet and peaceable life in all godliness and honesty."* (KJV) Who would not want to live in peace? One would wonder about someone, especially a Christian, who loves war and contention, whether at a personal or at a national level. Although there are many wars fought in the Scriptures, it is interesting to note that when eternity unfolds after Jesus returns to reign, there is going to be peace even among the beasts. (Isaiah 11:6) The fall of apartheid in South Africa is one of our primary modern day examples. Watchmen-intercessors, not only in South Africa but all across the world were in constant intercession for this ungodly system to change. I remember being in local and international gatherings where intercessions were made with tears for the people of South Africa during that period. It has been a delight to travel to this region and to see the respect shown to the leader of that freedom movement, Nelson Mandela, who became a prisoner then the President of that nation.

Idi Amin Dada was the third President of Uganda from 1971 to 1979. Although a cruel dictator who led his country to catastrophe, he still needed prayers. Uganda needed prayers. The Christians never stopped praying. Not only was this ruler guilty of genocide, over 300 thousand murders connected to him, but he needed to be stopped. Man was afraid to stop him but divine intervention was capable. The country was freed of his dictatorial reign when he went into exile.

Since then, Uganda has experienced a revival that is recorded by George Otis in the *'Transformations II'* Video/DVD Series. A revival that many have attributed to the prayers that were intensely lifted up to God at that time.

Jackson Senyonga, an international prayer leader and senior pastor of the 22,000-member Christian Life Church in Uganda's capital city of Kampala, explains how God brought transformation to Uganda.

> *In Uganda, we got our revival through devastation. The suffering of the people was beyond description, and no one came to our rescue. But God used the opportunity to wake a nation from its spiritual coma.*

> *A remnant of believers went into the jungle. They gathered in underground caves. In desperation they prayed, "Lord, we don't know what to do. But you know." These people prayed continuously. They prayed desperate, deep, consistent, groaning prayers that never took no for an answer. They prayed until they saw a change.*

> *Today, researchers say Uganda is one of the most transformed nations on the face of the earth. We've seen God transform the political system, the marketplace, and the church.*

> *[www.Christianity.com]*

1 Timothy 2:3-4 informs us that it is God Who "will have all men to be saved, and to come unto the knowledge of the truth". (NKJV) This includes our national and civic leaders. God wants those who have chosen to serve the nation at the political level to make it into heaven too. Kenneth E. Hagin in commenting on this verse had this to say:

*As Christians, we should be concerned about our nation, but we shouldn't put politics before Christ. We should be interested, and we should vote and do all we can to have good government. But the main thing we should do is pray... It's so easy to criticize, but the Bible never tells us to do that. I've found that it's hard to criticize someone you're praying for. And the same is true when we're praying for our government leaders. Christians have the authority, power, and know-how to turn things around in government if we'll take advantage of it. But we'll not change things by criticizing; **we'll change them by getting on our knees and interceding.***

(Kenneth E. Hagin (rhema.org)

National and Civic Leaders to pray for include: Royal family / Governor General; President / Prime Minister; Opposition Leaders; Congress/Cabinet; Members of Parliament; Chief Justice; State / City / Community Leaders and other Local Officials; Heads of Armed Forces. If our prayer is for their salvation, then if they all get saved, we would have Righteous Governments, Righteous Opposition and Righteous Leaders in all segments of society.

Apart from interceding for leaders, there are other aspects of a nation that need to be covered in prayer and on a regular basis. These include idolatry, crime and violence, the economy, the children and youth, the taxation system, the justice system, the legislative process, the poor, widows and orphans, cults and the occult, the media, educational system.

Another way to sum up the areas of prayer is what Bill Bright, founder of Campus Crusade, and Loren Cunningham, founder of Youth With a Mission, in 1975, termed as "The seven mountains of influence in culture". These are business, government, media, arts and entertainment, education, the family and religion (www.7culturalmountains.org). Intercessors are not permitted to pray their will or opinion into these areas but must be guided by the Word of God. There are many Scriptures that can be directly applied to pray over a nation and some by using the principles. Here are a few.

- Psalms 2:8 – God encourages His people to "Ask of me, and I shall give thee the heathen for thine inheritance, and the uttermost parts of the earth for thy possession." (KJV) This is the Scripture that gives us the confidence we need to pray.

- Ps 22:27 - We can pray for "All the ends of the world" (which includes our nation) to *"remember* and *turn* unto the LORD: and … shall *worship* before thee." (KJV)

- Proverbs 21:1 – The hearts of our leaders to turn to God since "The king's heart is in the hand of the Lord, Like the rivers of water; He turns it wherever He wishes." (NKJV)

- Eze 14:6 - Every nation must be dealt with in the area of idolatry, in whatever form it shows up. We must pray for God to move upon our nation to "Repent , and turn yourselves from your idols." (KJV)

- Joel 3:14 – Prayer must be in earnest for "the multitudes in the valley of decision" to turn their lives over to Jesus before it is too late.

- Hab. 2:14 - We must be zealous for the earth to be filled with the "knowledge of the glory of the Lord" since it is only then that we will see God being truly glorified not only in our own nation but in the nations of the world.

- Mt 24:14 – since it is God's heart that none should perish but all be brought to the knowledge of Christ (2 Peter 3:9), our prayer then should be "that the gospel of the kingdom may be preached in all the world".

- Mk 12:36 – God has some demonic enemies that He must subdue in order for His kingdom to come so we need to pray "and make Your enemies to be Your footstool."

- Jn. 16:8 – God needs to "convict the world of sin, and of righteousness, and of judgment". (NKJV)

- 2 Corinthians 10:5 – Our effectual fervent prayers for the nation should be "Casting down imaginations, and every high thing that exalteth itself against the knowledge of God, and bringing into captivity every thought to the obedience of Christ;" (KJV)

- Phil 2:10 - We must be in prayer that from the top to the bottom of our nations, "every knee bow and every tongue confess that Jesus is Lord."

- I Timothy 2:1-2 – That all men be saved! A simple but profound prayer.

What an opportunity and a privilege to be given the divine unction and anointing to pray for and to steer the course of a nation. The history books may never record the names of intercessors; they may never receive any national accolades; the wounds of wars fought on the frontline of prayer may never be known by others but what pleasure to know that heaven records in the annals of time the men, women, youth and children who have effectively altered the course of their nations under divine guidance and authority through prayer.

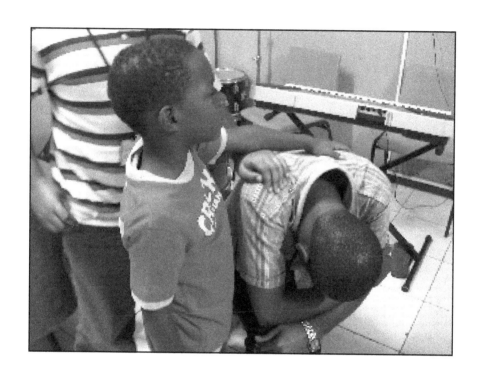

CHAPTER 9

Powerful Praying Children

When children are free to pray, they become history-makers.
Praying children had high visibility in great awakenings and
unusual moves of God in the past. With the spirit of supplica-
tion upon them, their prevailing prayer reportedly hastened
revival.

Esther Ilnisky

A BOOK OF this nature could not be written without hailing and
highlighting the young soldiers who are equally a part of the army of
watchmen-intercessors. The Scriptures have introduced us to some –
the child Samuel who "ministered unto the Lord" (1 Samuel 3:1) and
stayed in the presence of the Lord in the temple (1 Samuel 3:3). There
was young Jeremiah who was called to be a prophet to nations from
the time he was a child (Jeremiah 1:4-10); David who was described
by God as a man after His own heart. It is evident that David's zeal for
God and the things of God developed from he was a youth helping
with his father's flock (1 Samuel 16:11-13); Esther was a young girl
when she was chosen to be queen and before she could settle in her
new role, trouble arose in the kingdom forcing her to spiritually and lit-
erally stand in-the-gap for her people, the Jews (Esther 2:2, 8; 4:13-14).

In modern times, there have been many children, heroes unknown to many whose names have not been posted anywhere, but who have changed their communities and impacted their nations through prayer. One such account was shared at a Children in Prayer Consultation in India about a group of children, the Royal Kids in Chennai, India about 1000 of them living in a Home. These children are featured in a video, *From Trash to Treasure* [http://vimeo.com/53407135]. They are called the Royal Kids – intercessor praying children. They prayed that a dry, 100-foot well would be filled with water. The children marched and prayed. A fountain was released and is still flowing today. These Royal Kids have their own television programme, "Angels Voice" Royal Kids TV Program where they take prayer requests and pray for whoever is in need (www.royalkids.org). It was our privilege to see these children in action at their large Home in Chennai. They had flags of the nations all over. We were asked to find our flag and when we did, there were children waiting to pray with us for our nation. The children are leading their parents to the Lord, planting churches, prayerwalking their neighbourhoods daily and changing communities, cities and nations through intercession. This is one of those *'even when you see it you may not want to believe it but it is happening right before your very eyes'* occasions.

Returning from a consultation in Chennai, India in 2008, my husband and I were not just impressed by the testimonies that we heard and saw with our own eyes, of God's powerful work through praying children, but we were convicted to start the Children in Prayer in Jamaica on our return to Jamaica, to encourage and motivate our children to pray and see God at work. The children have since been in prayer. They have so many testimonies including radical changes in disruptive behaviour in school, provision for their families in times of need, provision for international trips to the United Nations, etc.

They prayed... they believed...they saw God's hand at work. These are testimonies that cannot be taken from them.

One cannot think about raising up children in prayer without giving credence to the general who started Esther Network International/ Children's Global Prayer Movement in Florida, USA. In 2002, this woman of God, consumed in and with the fire of the Holy Spirit and His heart and zeal for children, mandated the Jamaican intercessors, under divine unction, never to leave the children behind. This mandate became the burden of the National Intercessory Prayer Network of Jamaica/Prayer Centre of the Caribbean(NIPNOJ/P-COC), to ensure that all of its major gatherings for prayer – Intercessors Camps, weekly training of intercessors, All-night Prayer meetings had space for the children to pray. The Children in Prayer movement officially started in Jamaica after a team attended an intergenerational summit in India in 2008. Since then, even more emphasis has been placed on the extraordinary place that children have in prayer. A special rally, Let The Children Cry Hosanna, has become an annual event to ensure that the nation's children are able to get together with the adults to pray. Now this has spiralled into an entire outreach programme, Children Cry Hosanna, touching schools and children's homes. Kathryn Snider, the coordinator of this programme shares her story:

Around 2006, the Network (NIPNOJ) helped to host a chil-dren's prayer rally. We had invited Esther Ilnisky from Esther Network International / Children's Global Prayer Network to be our main speaker. The Lord had impressed upon me that morning the need to equip many of our children who hear gunshots daily. I knew many children, and adults, must be living in fear and terror. At that time some schools had to close or have their classes interrupted due to gun wars in their communities.

When I shared my idea with Esther in a pre-rally briefing, she said, "HOSANNA! The children need to shout "Hosanna" whenever they hear the gunshots! She continued and later taught that morning that the meaning of "Hosanna" is actually "God save us!" This was deep revelation to me as I had previously thought, as most of us do, that Hosanna only means "praise", thinking of Jesus riding in to Jerusalem on a donkey with the children shouting Hosanna.

That Saturday morning we had a powerful time of praying and shouting "HOSANNA" to the drum beat that imitated gunshots. I felt that not only was it God-ordained intercession but practice for the future. I had several testimonies after the prayer rally from mothers of young children who were faithful to shout HOSANNA when they did in fact hear gunshots.

Out of this experience, the " Let the Children Cry HOSANNA", the Prayer Network's annual children's prayer rally held every first Saturday in May in Kingston and every last Saturday in May in Montego Bay, was born.

In Jakarta, Indonesia, from May 14-18, 2012, the World Prayer Assembly had thousands of intercessors gathered from all across the globe. Many were ministry leaders from about 220 nations hosted by Indonesian and Korean prayer movements. As the adults met, the youth and children had their own meetings. They too came from all the continents to assemble because the organizers, the International Prayer Council (IPC) believe that this generation is critical to God's plan and they don't have to be any particular age to be used of God. God is raising up the younger generation to become cutting-edge leaders in the global prayer and mission movement. *Youth leaders, youth and children made up one-third of the participants,* and they helped to plan and lead that assembly as partners. It was an awesome encounter to behold the intergenerational sessions with youth and children praying for adults and vise-versa. The gathering spanned four generations. John Robb, chairman of the IPC lives the following statement that he made in the book, *Let The Children Pray*.

> *Investing in children through mentoring and encouraging them in a life of prayer is one of the most strategic things we can do as followers of Christ...The Children in Prayer movement that is now spreading to the ends of the earth is more a "God-thing" than anything else I know. (p.20)*

This was only one of many international intergenerational events hosted by the IPC with heavy financial and spiritual investment in the lives of children. Esther Ilnisky has been training many in raising up children in prayer for decades. Many children prayer networks have been spawned from the work of prayer generals like her and John Robb of the IPC along with their teams. What is God saying to the nations about our children? Esther Ilnisky usually asks this question in her seminars and workshops. Is there a baby Holy Spirit and an adult one? Pointing to the fact that the same works that the Holy Spirit does through an adult, He can and will do through a child. She took time to exhort and challenge the Body of Christ in her book, *Let The Children Pray,* that children can do much for God in prayer. She asks these thought provoking, mind-boggling questions that force one into a Selah moment:

- *Are children's powerful prayers being aborted today?*

- *Do our godly children have the right and the freedom to confront the spirits of this present darkness that are out to destroy them?*

- *In trying to shelter our children from the world, might we in reality be leaving them vulnerable to it? (p 44)*

We don't have to think too hard to answer these questions since we can recall as children being used / attacked by the Enemy – forces of darkness. These forces are no respecter of age or developmental stage. They pounce on very small and older children. They use and abuse them in the occult world, in military training, in human trafficking and the list goes on. The truth is, supernatural enablement, whether by God or demons have no age limit. Jeremiah was called, appointed and anointed from his mother's womb. (Jeremiah 1:5) The approach God takes with this child could be instructive to us who are trying to "protect" our children from going too deeply into the things of God and being baptized too young.

First of all, God spoke to a child, Jeremiah. (Jeremiah 1:4). This was not the first time in the Scriptures that He did so since the child Samuel also heard Him speak. (1 Sam 3:1, 10) "Now the Lord came and stood and called as at other times, "Samuel! Samuel!" And Samuel answered, "Speak, for Your servant hears." (NKJV) In both accounts the children not only heard God speak but answered and listened to what God had to say to them. Does it seem impossible to us that God could still be doing this all over the world? Does it seem even more improbable that God could be calling, appointing and anointing our own children, inside our house?

Secondly, God uses terminology to this child, Jeremiah, of the sort that one would want to break down when speaking to a child – formed, sanctified, ordained and prophet to the nations. Is this highlighting a peculiar knowledge that God has of children to which many adults need to pay attention? The God of the universe makes no mistakes. God's response to Jeremiah's reason for not wanting to be used by Him, "I cannot speak: for I am a child" (1:6 - KJV) is even more earth-shattering. In addressing this child, God does not allow Jeremiah to flounder because he is not yet an adult, but rather He calls Him to militant obedience.

"But the Lord said to me:"Do not say, 'I am a youth,' For you shall go to all to whom I send you, And whatever I command you, you shall speak."

(v 7- NKJV)

God however, in His compassionate nature, comforts the child's heart encouraging him not to be afraid. The main reason, "Papa is with you." When children know that their Dad is around, they usually feel safer and stronger. So he was told not to be afraid "of their faces", the very thing that intimidates most children, the looks on adults faces. God's promise was that "Papa will fight for you". He would be delivered.

Thirdly, God acts in a way that many adults believe He only does with older people. In Jeremiah 1:9, the LORD puts his hand on Jeremiah's lips and places His words in his mouth. How many adults reading this would not wish to have such an encounter with God? To have such an ordination from that point onwards, is divine unction to function and divine words to be heard by others through you? If the terminology before was thought to be too "adult", what God says next is even more disquieting. He now lays a mandate on this child that many adults are still attempting to carry out within their own call:

"See, I have this day set you over the nations and over the kingdoms, To root out and to pull down, To destroy and to throw down, To build and to plant."

(Jer. 1:10-NKJV)

Be reminded that this is the only Wise God who is addressing Jeremiah. The Omniscient One who is rolling out these instructions knowing fully well, Jeremiah's capabilities and the fact that he, despite his age, would succeed since it is divine presence that guarantees success.

My Own Story

I remember as a child simply falling in love with Jesus. A passionate Sunday School teacher, Sis. Chaise, was responsible for me becoming enamoured not with her but with Jesus. She spoke of Jesus as if He were her friend. She animatedly taught us how good and how great He was. I was so in-love with this Jesus that I could not afford to miss one Sunday School class, not for the prizes that I constantly got for attendance and participation but because this was feeding something in my young soul. I was getting very close to giving my life to Him by the time I was 11 years old but something happened. I was given a role in a Christmas production which was admittedly an enviable part - narrator for the entire play. I was the only one who spoke. I noticed that other persons in the production, some older than I was, were not pleased. They started a rumour that devastated me when I heard. I backed away from them and then from Church.

The next few years were ones of backward moves. However, there were some things that my Sunday School teacher taught me about Jesus, prayer and serving God that I could not get out of my head, even when I found myself running with the wrong crowd; seeking entertainment in the wrong places and generally wasting time while in High School. I kept praying and God would deliver me out of all types of situations – even dangerous, abusive situations. So it was not very difficult when at the age of fifteen, when I was introduced to that Lovely Man who my Sunday School teacher spoke so expressly about, that I threw my arms around Him and cried, "I need you... I need you...I need you!" That was my "sinner's prayer"; a simple cry from deep within. Whatever the young lady who was witnessing to me saw, led her to ask, "You just gave your life to the Lord, didn't you?" My answer was in the affirmative. What was interesting is that I had refused to pray with her only a few moments before because of fear. Fear? Yes. I had witnessed someone being delivered from demonic oppression only a few minutes before she walked up to me and began to inquire about the state of my soul.

By the time I reached home, I fell on my knees in prayer and it seemed like I have not gotten up since. Whatever happened to me after was charted by prayer, whatever the situation whether past disappointments, present challenges or future expectations. By this time the realization hit me that in my search for love and happiness, I had wasted my time in school and exams were around the corner. I had to do something. That something began with prayer! God answered by allowing me to pass enough subjects to enter 6th form on probation. I prayed again that I would be accepted fully by my performance. He answered again. I even became a student leader. I began meeting with another leader, who is still a friend and prayer partner today, each morning at her home prior to going to school. She and I spent time praying for our school friends; praying about the school affairs; praying for our Head Mistress; praying for our backslidden friend who we had the privilege of watching her life turn right back around to serving the Lord. We began to see changes in our High School. Students giving their lives to the Lord. Teachers were being impacted. A weekly Bible Study group formed which we led as students and other changes having to do with the organization of the programmes in the school occurred.

For about four months right after these things were happening, I got close to an adult who was involved with a cult. The Lord spoke to me (I knew His voice by then) and I knew what the Scriptures said about being unequally yoked, but I was disobedient. One of the first signs of God's displeasure was that I could no longer pray as I used to. For those months, no matter what time I woke up, the moment I went to have my devotions, I would fall asleep almost immediately. Something was wrong (James 1:15). Attendance at the Bible Study began to dwindle. My soul began to feel dry and thirsty! One Saturday afternoon when we all should be meeting to practice our art in the Art Room as we had been doing for months, I was the only one who turned up. While painting, the Lord visited and told me clearly, "You must get out of that relationship or you will become just like her." I had known by then that she was religious but not Christian and that the group she belonged to was anti-Christ! I broke down and wept in repentance. I knew that this had to be followed by active obedience, no matter the cost – no matter how much it hurt me or others! I will not say that it was easy. It was one of the most painful things that I had to do as a teenager but I loved Jesus more; and my Christian friends who were now more than concerned about my walk, stepped in to back me with prayer.

As a nineteen-year old student in college, I was faced with a bill for my fees that should have been paid at the beginning of the term. This was the second week. I was in faith for the provision. I had to face the administration department. It was not nice. I was embarrassed. Again I turned to what I knew to do as a child and now as a teen – Prayer. I was invited to a Dorm Prayer meeting that afternoon but did not want to attend. I wanted to stay on my knees but God spoke to me and said, "Don't pray away your faith." I understood what He was saying. I got up and joined the meeting. After the meeting I got a call from one of my leaders who wanted to meet with me on the college campus immediately. He was there in a jiffy. He flew open his briefcase, popped out his cheque book and exclaimed, "God spoke to me today. He said a father takes care of His children." My leader went on to make inquiries about my fees. I told him how much I owed. He wrote a cheque for what was owing, then said to me with a fatherly command: "Whenever this is due you let me know and don't let me have to ask you!" I felt like saluting and saying, Yes Sir! I was overjoyed!

God had answered prayer again. This meant that for the four years of my college life, my fees were paid, and paid on time. When I was an exchange student to Fort Wayne, Indiana, for my junior year, the fees covered the exchange student from the USA. It was too late by then to convince me as a youth that God could not or does not hear and answer prayer.

My husband, Devon Harbajan, was also saved as a child at 10 years old. Growing up on a military base, he began witnessing to other children. He was president of Interschool Christian Fellowship (ISCF) and started teaching Sunday school at age 11. He started teaching Vacation Bible School (VBS) at age 13 and was leading Sunday School Ministry by age 14. At that time over 120 children were in attendance. He began planning and leading camps and retreats for young people at age 18, and remained involved in Christian camps from that time to present as Director of the Children in Prayer Camps of NIPNOJ. He was part of the leadership of University and Colleges Christian Fellowship (UCCF) while at University of the West Indies and has been part of the leadership of church and para church organizations since the age of 14.

He is only one example of many children in modern times who God called, equipped and used from a tender age. It is not strange that his ministry has developed along the lines of raising up children in prayer as he knows, by his own example, that one is never too young for a mighty God to use. Devon offers us some guidelines when ministering to children in the area of prayer. Intercessors who are also children workers should pay close attention to this section.

Guidelines for Raising Up Children in Prayer

1. Recognize that the same Holy Spirit that operates in you as an adult is in operation in children who make themselves available to Him and obedient to his instructions. Therefore the same *spiritual gifts* that operate in adults can operate in children and God can use them to communicate a revelation from Him, discern spirits, heal and work other miracles as well.

2. Although children share the same Holy Spirit, they are still children and so the Holy Spirit expresses Himself through them *age-appropriately*. They don't just suddenly become mature and responsible because God is using them. They will still express themselves as children; they will still be playful, easily distracted, etc.

    Allow them this freedom to be themselves. I remember on so many occasions during prayer time, while waiting on the Lord, God gave a word of knowledge or revelation to a child who seemed distracted and not paying attention. The child delivered the word and then went right back to being distracted.

3. Encourage children to pray with adults and *publicly*. Don't see their prayers as any less than adults. In fact, many times, their prayers are heard above and beyond that of the adults because of the sincerity, child-like faith and innocence. During prayer times if you ask someone to pray and a child volunteers, don't ignore them, allow them to pray. Also if they are the only volunteers don't feel that you have to have an adult pray as well, because the child's prayer is not long enough or loud enough.

4. *Model* prayer to your children. Pray about every situation that

they encounter. If you are travelling and your child points out a homeless man, explain to him that God's wish is for us to prosper and then lead him/her in a prayer for the man. Do the same if he points out a policeman, a soldier or just an ordinary person. Let them develop the habit of praying for others who they encounter.

5. Keep a *prayer journal* and if your child is old enough, encourage them to keep one too. Record the prayers prayed and note the answers to prayer.

6. *Celebrate* answered prayers. *Testify* about it; don't keep it a secret. Let your child and others see that God answers prayers.

7. The typical children's workers are not usually trained or cultured to expect children to enjoy prayer, to pray seriously and enter a deep meaningful worship experience with God. They need to be re-cultured and re-tooled by exposure to what God is doing among the children in places like India, Africa, Indonesia, etc.

8. Children do not want to be entertained; they want a *deep* and *meaningful* relationship with God, the same as adult do.

9. Allow the children *freedom* to express themselves in worship. Don't force them to be quiet and still. If they wish to dance let them dance. If they are clapping off-beat, let them clap. They will soon learn to clap in rhythm. As long as their expression of worship is decent and orderly, i.e. not disruptive, allow them.

10. Prayer is not just talking to, but also *hearing from God*. Develop a habit in our children of always pausing to listen for, and expect an answer from God after every time of

prayer. Besides speaking, they can write, draw or find some creative way to express what God has said to them.

JON'L'S TESTIMONY

My name is Jon'l Ruddock. I am 9 yrs. old. I started having bahavioural problems when I was in Kindergarten 5. I would refuse to listen and would bawl when spoken to. I had to be transferred from one class to another but still the same. I was at the Principal's office more often than I care to remember. The school assigned me a counselor but that did not help. I gave my life to Jesus when I was in grade 2. Did I improve? No! **I got worse**. Mom and Dad began to take me to another counsellor but still I got worse. I was turning over my desk, throwing myself on the ground and being very disruptive. My grades fell so badly I went from High Honors to just merit then to just regular. Was I ashamed of myself? Yes I was. Did I feel bad about my behavior? I felt terrible. I thought I was the worst person alive. I prayed and prayed but no change. I was frustrated, my family was frustrated my teachers and my classmates were frustrated. I felt like a monster. I did not want to live. I wanted to die.

In September when I started to tear up my books and be rude to my teacher, my Mom decided that this was it. We cannot go on like this! No more counselors she said. No more calls from school. It's time to take a stand. Mom said it was time for *fasting*. We all had to fast (even my little sister). We prayed and read the bible. Mommy and Daddy prayed for each of us and anointed us with oil. When we got hungry, we prayed some more and read the bible some more. We were fasting until midday. My sister and I were watching the clock counting off the minutes, until finally! Twelve midday.

"Foood!" we cried. Mommy said, "NO!" We had to pray again and close the fast properly. This was done and we dashed to the kitchen.

In the evening we went to "Children in Prayer" with Aunty Maria and Uncle Devon. They prayed for us again. Every night I would pray and ask God to help me to behave.

God really helped me. I was so well behaved for the month of October that I won student of the month for my class. I was so happy. I could hardly wait to tell my parents. When I got my report in December, I was back on the Honor roll. I am so thankful to God. He really answers prayers.

I know I can do all things through Christ who gives me strength. THE BIBLE ALSO SAYS WE OVERCOME BY THE BLOOD OF THE LAMB AND THE WORD OF OUR TESTIMONY. I HAVE OVERCOME.

(Jon'l Ruddock, Children In Prayer, Jamaica)

Now that you have been enlightened; now that you have been reminded; you must act to ensure that the children in your home or fellowship, as well as those who minister to them also get this message that God wants to use children now, not just to prepare them to minister when they become adults but He has already called many, anointed and appointed them to do various works of ministry --- NOW!

CHAPTER 10

Dealing with Curses Through Intercession

God the Father is now raising up the banner and calling forth those who will not be afraid to walk and operate in His power and anointing to set these kinds of captives free from the extreme demonic areas they may have fallen into.

[www.bible-knowledge.com]

I HAVE DECIDED to include a chapter dealing with breaking curses in the personal lives of watchmen-intercessors as well as intercessors having the knowledge of what to do to assist others in getting freedom from bondages through generational and other types of curses. From the outset, let it be known that this is not an attractive topic for many believers who prefer to believe that once saved you are immediately free of all curses. I have had too many experiences witnessing the opposite in my over three decades of walking with the Lord, to entertain this myth. It is my hope that this chapter will highlight the unseen barriers in our lives that seem resistant to prayer; the cloud over our heads that seem to remain even while others are receiving sunshine; the invisible ceiling on which we thump our heads every time we attempt to climb higher in God; that invisible hand/personality that seems to block our pathway, pushing us backwards as we seek to move forward in our purpose.

What is a curse? This word occurs about 230 times in the Bible in various forms but there are 36 Old Testament occurrences of this word as a noun. There are different verbs used for the term "to curse": *qalal*, occurs 82 times in the Hebrew Old Testament and frequently includes the idea of "cursing" or "making little or contemptible" (Exod. 21:17); The verb *arar* occurs 60 times in the Old Testament beginning in Genesis 3:14-17 where the serpent and the ground were cursed after sin entered the world. It is also a pronouncement of judgement on those who break covenant (Deut. 27:15-26). Apart from God using curses to judge, which only He has the right to do, pagans used curses to deal with their enemies, hence Balak soliciting Balaam to "curse this people" referring to the Israelites (Numb. 22:6). Israel also had ceremonial "water that causes the curse" which would cause sickness and deformity to come upon a woman who was guilty of adultery (Numbers 5:18-22).

One could point out that Jesus dealt with curses while He hung on the cross (Galatians 3:13; Deut. 21:23). This is a fact. However, earlier on, Paul had asked a potent question of the same Galatians, "You crazy Galatians! Did someone put a hex on you? Have you taken leave of your senses? Something crazy has happened, for it's obvious that you no longer have the crucified Jesus in clear focus in your lives. His sacrifice on the Cross was certainly set before you clearly enough." (Gal. 3:1- The Message). Keep in mind that this address was to Christians. In the New Testament, the compound, *epikatar-asthai*, now translates from the Old Testament use of the term curse. In the same way that Jesus has dealt with sickness and so now, "by whose stripes you were healed" (1 Peter 2:24 - NKJV) yet we do become ill and have the need to pray, fast and seek spiritual intervention to receive the manifestation of this healing, Jesus has also redeemed us from curses but we have to seek deliverance, being now empowered by Him, to break curses. It is a done deal but not an automatic manifestation.

A curse, according to Merriam-Webster Dictionary is:

- *a prayer or invocation for harm or injury to come upon one : imprecation*

- *something that is cursed or accursed*

- *evil or misfortune that comes as if in response to imprecation or as retribution*

- *a cause of great harm or misfortune*

  [www.merriam-webster.com/dictionary/curse]

Please note that the word "curse" could also refer to the evil or misfortune that comes in response to such prayers and incantations. Prov. 18:21 is very specific in enlightening us that "death and life are in the power of the tongue."(ASV) The apostle James warns us of the dangers of the tongue. He uses very strong language to impact upon Christians how careful we ought to be with the use of our tongues.

> *"Even so the tongue is a little member and boasts great things. See how great a forest a little fire kindles!"*

> *(James 3:5-NKJV)*

Apart from the tongue, curses can come through the use of objects (Numbers 5:11-13). Those who have been exposed to *witchcraft* have testified to the use of dolls with pins in places like Haiti to afflict human bodies; in obeah, a form of witchcraft, practiced in places like Jamaica; the use of a person's clothing to transmit a curse to them; and the use of various kinds of oils to break up marriages, torment people's minds, create failures, accidents, etc. Exodus 20:4 highlights another quick source of a curse and that is through an idol. This is whether the person is practicing idolatry or in possession of an image representing an idol. Sexual relationships have also been a vehicle of transmitting curses from one person to another. In an article on "Battle Prayer to Break a Generational Curse Line", the writer gives this testimonial which is not difficult for me to believe having heard many others in counselling sessions:

> *I have personally met several women who had carried de-mons into their married lives – all as a result of a curse line that had formed out between them and their natural mother or father who had been operating in one or more of these heavier types of transgressions against the Lord.*

> *[www.bible-knowledge.com]*

Proverbs 26:2 tells us that "A curse *without* cause shall not alight."(NKJV) What then would cause a curse to alight. If we can sum up the answer to this from the Scriptures in one word, that word would be Disobedience – especially to the laws of God. (Deut. 28:1-2, 15)

There is an author by whom I have been impacted in his writing on this topic of curses, along with a powerful testimony of life-changing deliverance by a reader of his book. This author is the late Derek Prince who wrote among many other books, *Blessing or Curse: You Can Choose.* Derek Prince gives some other reasons why curses can come upon, even the Christian:

- False Gods - Exodus 20:1 – 5 (God has pronounced a curse on idol worshippers down to the 3rd. and 4th. generations. (Deut. 27:15; Romans 1:20 – 23) The OCCULT is included!

- Various Moral and Ethical Sins - Deut. 27:15 Disrespect for parents (Ephesians 6:1 – 3) All forms of oppression and injustice especially directed towards the weak and helpless. All forms of illicit or unnatural sex (Deut. 27:20 – 23; Leviticus 18:22)

- Anti-Semitism = hatred or cursing of Jewish people. Genesis 12:2 – 3; Numb. 24:9

- Legalism, Carnality, Apostasy – Jer. 17:5f. - trusting in flesh; departing from God. (Galatians 3:10)

- Theft, perjury, robbing God - Zech. 5:1 – 4; Haggai 1:4 – 6; Malachi 3:8 –9 - "… you are cursed with a curse, for you have robbed Me."

- Authority Figures - curses coming from husbands knowingly or unknowingly cursing wives (Gen. 31:32 ; 35:16 – 19); Fathers their children; teachers their students; Pastor/Elders their members.

- Self-imposed Curses - Matt. 12:36-37 – "Will give account of every idle word spoken" (Prov. 6:2; Matt. 27:20 – 26).

- Servants of Satan - Numbers 22-24 - Balak hired Baalam to pronounce curses upon Israel.

- Soulish Talk - gossip; malicious chatter or rumour about others (Jas.3:6)

- Soulish Prayers – Prov. 28:9 – "…even his prayers shall be an abomination" – if we ignore God's principles and offer up prayers contrary to them.

The prophet Malachi in his final verses in Scripture notifies his listeners that Elijah the prophet is coming and "he shall turn the heart of the fathers to the children, and the heart of the children to their fathers, lest I come and smite the earth with a curse." (Malachi 4:5-6 - KJV). The question could be asked: What if these hearts don't turn, will a curse come upon the nations where this is an issue? It is evident that if this should happen, generations will be impacted. Curses can have their sources in previous generations. These curses however can be compounded by the sinful actions of subsequent generations. Curses can also have nothing to do with past generations but with personal choices (Deuteronomy 30:19). However a curse comes, it is clear that the effect can be upon an individual but may extend to families, communities and even nations. Someone has to do something to appeal to God to cancel a curse and thus to halt its effect.

Derek Prince in looking at Malachi 4:5-6, points out that:

Malachi has put his finger on the most urgent social problem of our contemporary culture and it is the outworking of a curse which is responsible for the agonies of strife-torn homes, broken marriages and disintegration of the families." (p 52)

Prince also alerts his readers to the various ways that curses can afflict people. Much of his information comes from Deuteronomy 28. Here is Prince's seven indications of a curse listed in his book which I have summarized:

- *Mental/Emotional Breakdown - madness; confusion of heart or mind; anxiety. (vs. 28, 34)*

- *Repeated or Chronic illness, especially if hereditary – being plagued with diseases (vs. 21 – 28)*

- *Barrenness, a tendency to miscarry or related female problems. - failure to menstruate, conceive; cysts, tumours; miscarriages, etc. (v. 18)*

- *Breakdown of Marriage and Family alienation - v 41. ...sons and daughters shall go into captivity. (Malachi 4:5-6)*

- *Continuing financial insufficiency (vs. 17, 29; 47 – 48). Absolute poverty - "...in hunger, in thirst, in nakedness and in need of **all** things.*

  > *"Poverty is having less than all you need to do God's will in your life." (p 54)*

- *Being "accident prone" - prone to 'freak' accidents, constantly falling down, etc.*

  > *"It almost seems that there is an invisible, malicious force working against such people. At critical moments, it trips them, or causes them to stumble, or impels them to make a rash, unpremeditated move. Typically, such a person will exclaim, "I don't know what made me do that!" (p. 57)*

- *A history of Suicides and Unnatural or Untimely deaths. One common symptom is that people set dates for their own deaths – knowing that all the men in their family die young. Continually overshadowed by failure and frustration and his life is snuffed out at an untimely age. (p.15)*

PASTOR HARRY WALCOTT'S STORY

After years of being a Christian I was at a stage of wondering what in the world was happening to me. I was struggling trying to make the business I had started some years before work.

I was struggling spiritually and was spending long hours just trying to make ends meet without much success. It was then that I started to cry out to the Lord for help.

I fasted and prayed that the Lord would show me what was happening and how to deal with the situation. It was then that the Lord began to direct my attention to the passage of scripture in 2 Samuel 21 in which King David inquires of the Lord as to why Israel was suffering the prolonged drought that they were experiencing. The Lord told him that it was because of what Saul had done to the Gibeonites in killing them, in his zeal, after Israel had made a covenant agreeing that they would not do so. Israel was now suffering under a curse because they, through Saul's reckless actions, had broken the covenant.

I became very interested in this passage of scripture as my attention was constantly drawn to it by the Holy Spirit. I began to see how the wrong words/actions of an authority figure can affect a person/community even though the event took place years before and even though the main person who was directly responsible (in this case King Saul) had been dead for some time.

Somehow I seemed to know that this scripture held the answer for my life and what I was going through at the time but did not know how to apply it. It was at this stage that I became aware of the book "Blessing or Curse: You Can Choose" by Derek Prince. I had purchased it from a Christian book store which subsequently informed me when I returned to buy another copy,, that they did not stock that book. I found this quite puzzling and amazing and could only conclude that God was at work to get this book into my hands.

This book was a tremendous blessing. Derek Prince in his profound yet easy to understand way, opened my understanding of how blessings and curses operate and gave me insight to what was operating in my life and how to deal with it.

Early in the book Prince makes the argument for believing that the pronouncement of blessings and curses can have real and lasting effects and can continue for generations. He makes the point that many people believe that blessings are a valid and acceptable concept but most are not so open to the reality of curses and their effects. However, he points out that positive elements always have a negative counterpart e.g. love and hate, light and darkness etc. If blessings are real then curses are also real.

The part that proved most helpful is the chapter that deals with what he calls "ecclesiastic curses." These are words spoken by a person who has a position of authority in the church e.g. apostle, prophet, pastor etc. over those under his authority. He pointed out how such individuals have been given the authority and great privilege of pronouncing blessings on the people they oversee but goes on to show how this power that has been given primarily as a blessing to the body of Christ can be used to curse. He gave an example of a fairly common occurrence in the church which was what opened my eyes to what had been working in my life over the past five years up to that time.

The example was of a person who informs his pastor that he has decided to leave that congregation. The pastor does not agree that this is God's will and may end by saying something to the effect that *"if you leave you will be out of the will of God and you will not prosper"*. These words amount to a curse and even if the pastor is ignorant of the dynamics at work, this curse still has the power to negatively affect the life of the person it is directed to. Case in point; Jacob ignorantly curses Rebecca who subsequently dies in childbirth (Genesis 31:32; 35:17-19)

This example of the pastor pronouncing the curse was very significant to me because similar words were spoken to me when I decided to leave the church I had been going to at the time. After this event I found it difficult to minister with the same kind of effect that I used to have. This and other areas of my life suffered until I recognized what was happening and was able to deal with it by repentance, prayer and positive declarations of faith of what Jesus has done for me. Now I have been able to walk in freedom and to minister being liberated as a pastor and intercessor.

(Harry Walcott, President, Jamaica House of Prayer, Jamaica)

Guidelines for Intercessors

If there is one set of persons who can be guilty of "soulish prayers" it is those who pray the most but pray unintelligently. That is with the wrong motives, the wrong disposition of the heart, or simply out of wrong information. There are therefore some key reminders for all who serve as watchmen-intercessors.

First of all, intercessors must daily remind themselves that we serve from a place of humility and in that position we seek to purify our motives for doing what we do. This is where we need the help of the Holy Spirit as outlined in an earlier chapter (Romans 8:26). If intercessors don't watch what they pray / how they pray, they are in danger of praying prayers that depreciate into ones that are demonic in nature according to James 3:15.

A second guideline is to guard against accusation in our prayers and seeking to control and manipulate others. In our humanity, and especially when we are in authority at whatever level, this is always a temptation to be aware of . This is where we can get into "witchcraft" praying, i.e. we use our tongues to set others on "fire" in the wrong way leading to devastating consequences. Prayers are often used as a medium to say things / reveal things that we don't want to say otherwise. It is pretty much similar to how someone in a drunken state can utter accusations that they are not brave enough to do when there is sobriety. The bible is clear that Satan is behind accusation of the brethren. (Rev. 12:10; Rom.8:33f; Isa. 54: 17) Prov. 11:9 - "The hypocrite with his mouth destroys his neighbour."(NKJV)

Thirdly, watchmen-intercessors must always be aware that curses can be operating in their own lives too, blocking them from achieving answers to prayers, especially for their personal lives and within their families. Whatever can ail any Christian can also oppress the intercessor and sometimes even more so since the intercessor is a dangerous instrument in the hand of God to bring down the Enemy's strongholds. (2 Cor. 10:4) Intercessors should carefully seek the Lord to break any childhood, generational or other curses that might be present. Sometimes, this might entail the intervention of a Minister or other intercessors in order to produce the breakthrough. The watchman-intercessor must never see deliverance as an evil or scornful endeavour.

However a curse comes, it is clear that the effect can be upon an individual but may extend to families, communities and even nations. Someone has to do something to appeal to God to cancel a curse and thus to halt its effect.

How to Reverse a Curse

- *Reassure* yourself of your position in Christ as a believer who has been sanctified through his blood.

- *Repent* of any known sin within your life / confess any sins that might be present in your family.

- *Revoke* the curse - renounce, denounce and cancel it; deal with any known or unknown covenants that might have been made with the powers of darkness. Renounce all contact with anything within the occult world, even with jewelry, figurines, etc. (II Cor. 6:14f)

- *Repeat* the Scriptures – those that reminds us of what Jesus has already accomplished (Isa. 53:4; Gal. 3:13)

- *Rverse* the effects of wrong confession – whatever was said by you or others that does not line up with Scriptures and as a result brought a curse must be renounced too.

- I Refuse to let up until every curse is broken and the effects removed from my life.

- *Radically* decide to walk in God's Word and in His ways. Refuse from here on to compromise with sin or make any pact with the powers of darkness / any of their emissaries.

A Prayer to Break Curses

Father of the whole universe and the One Who is in control of everything that happens in the heavens, within the earth and in the realms of principalities. I come to you in the Name of Jesus; the only Saviour of the world and the only One who can bring true deliverance to mankind by the shedding of His blood on the cross at Calvary. I thank you that I have been redeemed and bought with the precious price of His blood which now gives me every legal right to be called a son of God.

I *Repent* of any known sin within my life; I confess that I have sinned by .... I now repent of these sins which have created open doors to the Enemy of my soul, Satan. I confess too the sins of my family which are .... As I confess these sins, I ask your forgiveness for offending your holy nature and that you now close every door in my life/my family that makes us vulnerable to the curses of the Enemy.

I now Revoke every curse. I renounce, denounce and cancel every curse. I cancel any and every known or unknown covenants that might have been made with the powers of darkness. Where my forefathers have made any such covenants, through the blood of Jesus I now cancel these covenants and the speakings of these covenants are now made null and void. I renounce all contact with anything within the occult world, and rid myself and my family of any object that might be a medium that would connect me to the kingdom of darkness. (II Cor. 6:14f) *I Reverse* the effects of wrong confession – whatever was said by me, my family or anyone else that does not line up with Scriptures and as a result brought a curse. I renounced all of these confessions over my life/my family. I refuse to back down or back off from assaulting the Enemy.

Refuse to let up until every curse is broken and the effects removed from your life.

I thank you that it is written in Isa. 53:4-5 that He, Jesus, has borne our grief, and carried our sorrows: and he *was* wounded for our transgressions, he was bruised for our iniquities: the chastisement of our peace was upon him; and with his stripes we are healed. It is also written in Gal. 3:13 that Christ has redeemed us from the curse of the law, being made a curse for us: for it is written, Cursed *is* every one that hangs on a tree. Through this finished work of Jesus on Calvary, I hereby claim the deliverance that He has wrought for me.

I today rededicate my life and decide to walk in God's Word and in His ways. I refuse from here on to compromise with sin or make any pact with the powers of darkness / any of their emissaries.

CHAPTER 11

Intercession Is Not a Weird Affair

We are either in the process of resisting God's truth or in the process of being shaped and being molded by His truth.

Charles Stanley

FOR THE PAST two decades I have been burdened with the mistakes that have been made in the ministry of intercession. Mistakes in belief, in the execution of and in response to intercession. The cry has been heard on both sides of the fence. On the one hand, there are pastors and other church leaders who have experienced much frustration as they have sought to fulfill their responsibility in shepherding those members of their flock who are intercessors. They have complained of experiencing from rebellion to the threat of a church-split when they have allowed intercessors to freely operate in the congregation. On the other hand, intercessors have experienced being misunderstood, silenced and sometimes classified as "witch- hunters" and spooky. This chapter is intended to correct some of these painful experiences on both sides.

The truth is that every Church needs intercessors and the intercessory ministry is needed to stand and undergird all the ministries and ministry personnel in that Church. Intercessors need to have spiritual authority in their lives, pastors and elders, who can encourage, guide and bring discipline and correction. Satan has had a hay day in many fellowships as he has successfully brought about offences that have pushed leaders and intercessors apart. Some intercessors have fallen by the wayside because of some of these experiences.

Teresa Seputis explains this in an article, *"A Spiritual Checkup For Intercessors"*:

> *One of the strategies that the enemy will use against interces-*
> *sors is to try and get them to disqualify themselves. No one*
> *can "take an intercessor out" (or make them ineffective) more*
> *quickly and powerfully than that intercessor themselves. E.g.,*
> *the enemy wants to try and talk intercessors out of stepping*
> *up to the place of intercession. He tries to focus them on their*
> *failures, their inadequacies, etc. and convince them that they*
> *have no right to be praying/interceding because they are too*
> *much of a mess.*

> *[http://www.godspeak.net]*

Intercessors Are Not Spooky People

Contrary to what some may think, although within the activity of intercession one might be led of God to do things out of the ordinary, intercessors don't live spooky lives. I recall as a young intercessor praying and flailing my hands, moving my hand in a chopping motion, my finger pointing in different directions when I was praying under the unction of the Holy Spirit. I began asking myself many questions: Why am I doing this? Am I just being dramatic? Why does my body get so involved in prayer and most people seem to pray in a very controlled manner? It puzzled me but somewhere deep inside I knew that God was using me. As a seminary graduate however, I was schooled that the Scriptures should undergird whatever we do and should be the final authority.

It was while sitting in a meeting being led by prayer general, Esther Ilnisky, that I got the answer. She quoted from Ps. 144:1 which tells us that the LORD teaches my hands to war, *and* my fingers to fight / for battle. The lights came on in my head. Oh that is what this is all about! What a revelation. The God of the Universe uses the hands of His people to do spiritual warfare on His behalf. Sometimes my hands would shake or feel like they were on fire. It was heartening to know that God would use His people and empower them with His strength. He uses them, any part of their bodies that He chooses, to bring about His purposes on earth.

Another Scripture Esther used which was enlightening to me and also explains the manner in which God uses intercessors was Jeremiah 51:20:

> *"Thou art my battle axe and weapons of war: for with thee will I break in pieces the nations, and with thee will I destroy kingdoms."*

> *(KJV)*

I have also been led during a time of intense warfare in a congregation to use the drums as an instrument of war. Sometimes it sounds like guns in war. The level of energy and rhythm that comes out I know is not of me. So Psalm 149:6-9 shows us how high praises is linked to warfare! There is an act that Jesus did which Christians have not dubiously questioned but if one of His followers were to do the same, they would be doubted and perhaps labelled. In John 9:6, Jesus "spat on the ground, and made clay of the spittle, and anointed his eyes with the clay,."(ASV) Also in Mark 7:33, "Jesus and put his fingers into his ears, and he spat, and touched his tongue;" (ASV) Later, in the town of Bethsaida, Jesus healed a blind man. Again, the miracle was preceded by spitting: "and when he had spit on his eyes, and laid his hands upon him" (Mark 8:23-ASV). Jesus did not need physical or dramatic props to do miracles. In fact in many places He healed by just speaking the word and in the case of the woman with the issue of blood, His healing power flowed through his garment.

There is an overarching reason why Jesus did what He did and at the timing that He chose and it is what He Himself declared in John 5:19: Jesus gave them this answer: "Then Jesus answered and said to them, "Most assuredly, I say to you, the Son can do nothing of Himself, but what He sees the Father do; for whatever He does, the Son also does in like manner."(NKJV) So we can conclude from this passage that Jesus confined Himself to doing only what He already saw, with His spiritual eyes, the Father doing. So too with many intercessors. Their spiritual eyes have been sharpened to "see" what God is about to do and their spiritual ears to "hear" what the Spirit of God wants them to hear in the moment of interceding (Mark 4:9). Sometimes it comes in the form of a directive and at other times it is the end-result that is shown so the intercessor prays into being, what is visualized (Romans 4:17).

Having said this, it would be remiss if some of the mistakes that intercessors make in the activity of intercession were not pointed out for the sake of clarity, to bring mutual understanding and to correct the erroneous approaches and practises. Many mistakes have been made out of mere ignorance and some from having wrong models. Those genuinely called to this ministry with a heart after God will be willing to realign their thinking and transform their methodology in order to further please God.

Some Common Mistakes Intercessors Should Avoid

- **Super-spirituality** – a term being used in this context to describe those who may consider themselves *above others spiritually because they pray / fast more than others*. It is the sin
of the Pharisee which was exposed when compared to the
publican (Luke 18:9-14). This parable was spoken for those
who trusted in their own righteousness and despised others.
Prayers should never be done in a competitive manner or in
order to impress anyone about our spirituality. Such prayers
are soulish and will not be effective. At the foundation of this
is pride. The opposite of what should be the hallmark of an
intercessor.

- **Being a Mystery** - this points to the intercessor who may feel
that *the more mysterious his/her practice is in intercession,
the more persons will be awed by him/her*. The truth is that no
one should be seeking to be "awed". God is the only person
who should take centre stage when we are praying and any
results should only point to Him, giving Him all the praise
and glory and worship. So rolling the eyes in a particular way
to have persons on the edge of their seats; moving around as
if floating on air; imitating acts that one would see only on
horror movies or when observing spiritualists are actions that
should not be associated with the watchman-intercessor. An
intercessor does not need to employ the use of theatrics in
order to be respected in their role.

- **Witchcraft Praying** – this is the *type of praying fuelled by a
desire to control others*. It is not about praying God's will for
someone else's life but praying what the intercessor desires to
see happen. For example, if the intercessor is praying for an
engaged couple but would rather see one of those persons

engaged to his/her friend, that intercessor has to be careful that in praying, personal preferences don't interfere. The rule of thumb here is that all our praying should be to bring God's kingdom into the situation and to let His will be done – like it or not.

- **Being a Self-made Person** - this is a no *one can tell them what to do* attitude. They take their own counsel because they have "a straight line to God". This can be very harmful to an intercessor because no matter ones status in life; no matter how many hours one spends in the presence of God; in spite of the quantity of answers to prayers one receives; he/she has to be careful never to be a "lone-ranger". Other people's counsel matter. God will use the smallest child and the unschooled to speak to us. If we are imprudent and resist other's input into our lives, we could find ourselves soon becoming shipwrecks. After all, no one can truly boast of getting where they are spiritually or otherwise without in some way, others helping them. A spurning of fellowship with other Christians is a trap! A feeling of not needing to be under the covering of a Church fellowship is spiritual suicide.

- **An Above Deception / Cannot be Targeted Mentality** – whoever *believes that he cannot be deceived* is already deceived and those who consider themselves immune to the temptations of the Enemy could find themselves falling. The truth is there is a sober warning in the Scriptures to all believers who have the "Superman" syndrome. "Therefore let him who thinks he stands take heed that he does not fall. No temptation has overtaken you but such as is common to man …" (1Co 10:12 – 13 - NAS). The greatest evangelists can fall; the most powerful preachers can fall; the most effective intercessor can lose his grip.

- ■ ***A Rebellious Nature*** - this perhaps is the most disconcerting one for pastors and other authorities in the life of the intercessor. It is *a refusal to submit to the leadership of the fellowship* into which God has placed the intercessor. It is a type of passive aggressive, rarely overt resistance to being led. It usually comes out of a disposition of the heart that makes that intercessor, consciously or subconsciously believe that he/she has arrived in a position in God, is now hearing from God, knows more than those who are leaders in the fellowship and does not need to listen to or obey the instructions of those leaders. This is where intercessors can easily fall into deception because with this attitude towards the leadership God has set up over you, you no longer have the true covering of the Church. Satan recognizes this and is able to bring all types of calamities into that intercessor's life. Troubles and trials that come not as the normal testing that every Christian goes through but is designed for the disobedient, unruly, defiant, uncontrollable intercessor. The Bible exhorts every believer to submit to those who are in authority over us. (James 4:6-7; Hebrews 13:17; Ephesians 6:1-9; Romans 13;1-7) Matt Holcomb in an article, "Submission to Spiritual Authority" puts it this way:

> *Find a person who understands submission to authority and you'll see a person who is humble, full of love, unselfish, accountable, and personally responsible.*

> *Find a person who does not understand submission to authority and you'll see a person who is prideful, full of criticism, selfish, self-ruled, and spiritually irresponsible.*

> *[http://bromatt.wordpress.com/2009/06/22/*
> *submission-to-spiritual-authority]*

If you find yourself as a watchman-intercessor with the latter disposition, for whatever reason, act quickly, repent, ask your leader(s) forgiveness and make a decision in your heart to have a submissive attitude towards them (1 Thess. 5:12). This also applies to other authorities in the intercessor's life – dealing with a spouse, a boss, the Government, etc.

- *Anti-Social Tendencies* – not everyone is an extrovert by nature so this is not about being forced to become a social-butterfly. This is about using intercession to lock away oneself in order to avoid relating to people and as an escape from facing the world and the issues of life. It is being monkish when you have not been called to live a monastic lifestyle. Intercession is not a cover for not facing deep personal conflicts and neither is it an escape from tackling the issues that will confront us from day-to-day. Rather, it should be the first place that we turn in order to be equipped to take one-day-at-a-time.

- *Prayer Becomes An Excuse* – this is an "I will pray about it" response to everything not because of a dependency on God to lead us in every way but rather a distraction for ourselves and others to avoid taking action where it is obvious what we should do. Yes, prayer is the intercessors priority and primary focus but after praying, he/she should be prepared to act based on God's response to that prayer. Be prepared to listen to God's voice in every situation to see if it even requires prayer at all but rather to respond to His voice and act in faith. (James 2:16; 1 John 3:17)

- *Using Intercession to Gossip/Spread Rumours* – this is the scenario in which an intercessor reveals a confidential situation or other people's secrets while praying with others. This could happen while sharing prayer requests or within the prayer itself. Sometimes this is even used to impress others about how much knowledge we have about what is going on. Sometimes God will reveal to the intercessor what might be happening in other people's lives / within the Church. In such a situation we need God's wisdom to know what to do with this information. Should we pray it privately? Should we speak with the leadership and leave it there? Should we go to the person(s) involved as led of the Lord? Sometimes the intercessor might have heard a rumour, but doesn't have any evidence, and in the prayer meeting, he shares / prays repeating what he heard. This can create such confusion and damage to people's reputation, family life, ministry, business and integrity. Intercessors need to seek God's wisdom about what to share when they receive information or revelation through whatever medium.

- **Seeing Intercession As a Last Resort Ministry** – intercession should not be used by those who cannot do anything else such as preaching, teaching, etc. as a ministry to tag-along-to until he/she can get some recognition in another up-front ministry. Intercession is a lifestyle and for some a specific calling which should be taken seriously whether or not the intercessor gains an audience or is never recognized publicly. As one minister puts it, "Intercession does not equip you for the greater work, it is the greater work". This is where 2 Corinthians 4:1-2 must have effect in our lives.

> "Therefore seeing we have this ministry, as we have received mercy, we faint not; But have renounced the hidden things of dishonesty, not walking in craftiness, nor handling the word of God deceitfully; but by

manifestation of the truth commending ourselves to every man's conscience in the sight of God."

(2Cor 4:1-2- KJV)

This was the theme passage used in my Valedictory speech when graduating from seminary while using as my topic, "Faithfulness Regardless". This is my encouragement to all who have this precious ministry of intercession that we quickly deal with any sin that easily besets us and the weight that bogs us down and hampers the job we are called to do (Hebrews 12:1). If we are in error in any way, and which Christian has never erred; that we open our hearts and minds to the Lord for Him to undo any "garbage" we have collected along the way; any mud that has stuck to our "gospel shoes" and to plug up any penetrating holes that have been created in our armour from the darts of the Enemy. I exhort you to let us be faithful regardless! Let us confess our faults one to another and do what we do best, pray one for the other that we may be healed and delivered (James 5:16). Now that the pitfalls have been revealed and the Satanic traps exposed, let us together defeat the Enemy so that God's critical ministry, that of the watchman-intercessor, can stand.

CHAPTER 12

Restoring the Fallen and Wounded

You may think that your weakness disqualifies you for noble, strong, beautiful living, or for sweet, gentle, helpful serving. But really it's something which, if you give it to Christ, He can transform into a blessing, a source of His power.

J. R. Miller

HAVE I EVER been tempted to stop interceding? Have I ever become fearful in battle? Have I ever doubted my abilities to carry on in this ministry? Was I ever disappointed, wounded, bleeding, and screaming for help? To all of the above I respond in the affirmative. Yes...yes...yes! Intercession is hard work; walking out intercession is tough-ground trampling and fulfilling a ministry-mandate has sometimes been daunting and absolutely painful. Apart from the physical and spiritual exertion of agonizing in prayer, one faces the injuries that "come with the trade". A carpenter, no matter how skilled, could get stuck by a nail or splinter, struck by his own hammer and cut by his own saw. A medical doctor is prone to contract some of the very viruses that he sets out to heal. It is often said that a cobbler's family's shoes looks worse than others because theirs get left behind while he is busy fixing everyone else's.

It is a fact of life that ministry costs! Some pay a higher price than others and this is oftentimes God's choosing (Acts 9:16). However, the one thing God's people and the watchmen-intercessors can be assured of, is the fact that God will never give us more than we can handle (Cor. 10:13), in the same way that we would not ask a toddler to carry a refrigerator. God gives us our well fitted tests. They come neither oversized nor undersized no matter how we feel about them. Intercessors have been wounded in battle. Some have become casualties. Some have been limping along with their wounds while others have conceded defeat. This chapter is saying no to defeat. The boxing match is not over until God rings the final bell! One of the things that makes a boxing match interesting is the comeback that a boxer has after the last round, when he seems to be battered and on his last breath. When he is in his corner, sometimes with blood oozing out of his wounds, he is being patched up and prompted to get back in the ring. For the spectators, this seems like a wicked act. Why don't they just end the match? But this same boxer, beginning with wobbly feet and lifeless punches, suddenly gets a burst of strength, is revived to the core and beats his opponent to a finish! Who is the champion now?

The same prophet, Jeremiah, who was called, appointed and anointed from his mother's womb one day gave up. The battle was too much for him but it was not over for him.

Then I said, I will not make mention of him, nor speak any more in his name. But his word was in mine heart as a burning fire shut up in my bones, and I was weary with forbearing, and I could not stay.

For I heard the defaming of many, fear on every side. Report, say they, and we will report it. All my familiars watched for my

*halting, saying, Peradventure he will be enticed, and we shall
prevail against him, and we shall take our revenge on him.*

*But the LORD is with me as a mighty terrible one: therefore
my persecutors shall stumble, and they shall not prevail: they
shall be greatly ashamed; for they shall not prosper: their everlasting confusion shall never be forgotten.*

(Jeremiah 20:9-11 - KJV)

If such a great and choice prophet could bow under
discouragement, could that happen to one of us? Certainly. This is
the aim of this chapter. To allow the wounded / fallen watchmen
intercessors to be restored – to a spiritually healthy place; to a
fulfilling life of intercession; to the heights of ministry to which he/she
has been mandated by God. This chapter is to "hold your hand", lift
you up out of the doldrums, brush you off, provide you with spiritual
physiotherapy and get you back on your feet walking strongly again.

My Own Story

I have experienced some "midnight" events in my life that while
walking through them, I did not know how I or my ministry would
fare. If the Lord had not been on my side, there is no telling where I
would be today. One such event is the tragic loss of our 3+ year old
son in 2006. An experience that one would not want to see one's
worse enemy go through. Qowayne, our beloved, drowned because
someone carelessly left a manhole uncovered after clearing and
treating it.

It was unknown to the residents of our apartment complex that
this manhole, located in an area where the children played, was left
uncovered for 2 days. Our son, unknown to us, fell in it and was not

found until about 3 hours after. He was pronounced dead on arrival at the hospital. No one was held accountable since there were several persons involved in the process.

What would be some questions that an intercessor and minister of religion would ask having experienced such a horrible crisis? We did not ask the why me question but we certainly asked others. Why did you give us this child to take him away in such a horrible manner? Why were we not warned that this was to come? Where were the "prophets" who you usually speak to and some have spoken to us before about things that came to pass? Why did you not allow someone to see the cover off to avoid this? How do we explain to others the reason(s) that God has permitted such tragedy to befall our family? With all these questions floating in my mind, I felt feeble, faint and finished! How then did I come through this and the other "midnight" experiences? Here are some nuggets for your own restoration and, or to be considered while restoring others.

Healing for Novices And Veterans

There are some wounds that come merely from practicing intercession as a novice – the lack of knowledge is the source. There are others that come to both novices and veteran intercessors. Wherever one falls, it is time for healing.

- *God does the Restoring.* "For I will restore you to health And I will heal you of your wounds,' declares the LORD, 'Because they have called you an outcast, saying: "It is Zion; no one cares for her." (Jeremiah 30:17 - NAS). Though we may look to man to assist, it is only God who truly understands the reasons for and the depth of the wounds experienced. This is not a time to run from God but to run into Him. He has a balm for every wound (Jer. 8:22). Psalm 147:3 tells us that God "heals the brokenhearted and binds up their wounds." (NKJV) I have often said, and this is not a cliché: If I did not have God in my life I don't know what I would do!

- *Admission of Weakness and Affirmation of God's Strength.* One of the quickest ways to come into restoration is to have a realistic appraisal of oneself. I can fall. Having made that admission, it should be quickly replaced by what the Scripture says about your strength. "And he hath said unto me, My grace is sufficient for thee: for [my] power is made perfect in weakness. Most gladly therefore will I rather glory in my weaknesses, that the power of Christ may rest upon me. Wherefore I take pleasure in weaknesses, in injuries, in necessities, in persecutions, in distresses, for Christ's sake: for when I am weak, then am I strong. " (2 Corinthians 12:9-10 - ASV)

- *Dealing With Hard Core Forgiveness.* This is where many Christians get stuck. Letting go off offences. Yet this holding on will continually damage you and destroy your intercessory life. How do you forgive when your loved one's life was snuffed out through cruelty or carelessness? How does one rise up out of the ashes of abuse of any kind? How does one swim out of the waters of gossip and backbiting that threaten to overwhelm you? One has to begin with this simple but profound request in the Lord's Prayer: "And forgive us our sins; for we also forgive every one that is indebted to us (Luke 11:4 - NKJV). Unforgiveness, as I have heard it portrayed, is like someone drinking poison and believing that it is the other person who will be harmed from it. Bitterness is similar to the Matador vine in South America. This is how it was described in an article, *Bitterness: The Subtle Killer:*

The matador starts at the foot of a tree and slowly works its way up, sapping the life of the tree as it grows. When it reaches the top the tree is dead, and to crown itself it produces a single flower. The word matador in Spanish means "killer". Bitterness, just like the matador vine, can seem harmless at first. But it isn't long before its tendrils of resentment, malice, and hatred grab hold of the heart and eventually destroy one's health and kill the inner being.

[http://powered-by-adversity.com/adversity/barriers/ bitterness.php]

One of the things that watchmen-intercessors have to do is be brutally honest in prayer. This means calling a spade exactly what it is. If there is hate within our hearts for anyone, that is what it is called. We cannot water it down and call it dislike. We must identify the demons that torment us and address them in the power of the Holy Spirit. So if there is a spirit of unforgiveness operating, we should address and command such a spirit to be expelled from our lives.

- *Becoming Better Not Bitter.* This is a recognition that every experience, barring none, that God allows in our lives is for our betterment. Never for our ruination. Jeremiah 29:11 reminds of this that God's plans and thoughts for you are "thoughts of peace, and not of evil, to give you an expected end."(KJV) This is a mind-set that sustains one in all manner of circumstances and heartaches. This is the attitude that will allow us to truly come out of the murky waters of despair and disappointment and when you pass through the rivers, they will not sweep over you. When **you** walk through **the** fire, **you will not** be **burned**; the flames **will not** set **you** ablaze (Isaiah 43:2).

- *Grabbing Hold Again of God's Truths.* One of the quickest things we can be deceived into doing when we face deep hurt and disappointment is to let go of God's truth about Himself, about us, our situation, others, and the devil. We should be affirming the devil to be the liar and our enemy, and **not** God! This is recognizing that it is not merely "flesh and blood" that harmed us but the diabolical plan of the Enemy to steal, kill and destroy (John 10:10). This is an embracing of the truth that God is good every time, regardless of our experiences. What we experience cannot change His nature.

- *A 'So What' Attitude.* A former lecturer of mine challenged us one day to respond to the "What ifs" in our minds with "So what". This he recommended as an antidote to fear which often comes out of foreboding questions looming in our minds. This was food for thought. It worked for me. He was encouraging us to imagine the worst in any given situation and to respond with this question: So what? Used in this context, it is, so what if God does not / did not come through the way I expected Him to? So what if He allows me to go through a trial that I wish not to go through? Can I like the songwriter penned, after all I have been through, "I still have peace… joy…hope"? Yes I can.

- *A Refusal to Let Go My Purpose.* There is a distinct purpose that we were brought into this world to fulfill. This is a God-purpose that we do have the choice to fulfill or not. This is where we ought to be stubborn – to be resolute to fulfill that purpose whatever the high waters; whatever the fires blazing around us; whatever the earthquakes and tsunamis in our personal lives. A watchman-intercessor needs to value this purpose above every other instinct of self-preservation and the fallout that one experiences from the loss of a golden reputation. Both of which I had to fight to resurrect myself from over a decade ago when I experienced another "midnight" in my life. This resolution is akin to what Paul boldly declares in Romans 8:31-39:

> *What shall we then say to these things? If God be for us, who can be against us? He that spared not his own Son, but delivered him up for us all, how shall he not with him also freely give us all things? Who shall lay anything to the charge of God's elect? It is God that justifies. Who is he that condemns? It is Christ that died, yea rather, that is risen again, who is even at the right hand of God, who also makes intercession for us.*
>
> *Who shall separate us from the love of Christ? shall tribulation, or distress, or persecution, or famine, or nakedness, or peril, or sword? As it is written, For thy sake we are killed all the day long; we are accounted as sheep for the slaughter. Nay, in all these things we are more than conquerors through him that loved us. For I am persuaded, that neither death, nor life, nor angels, nor principalities, nor powers, nor things present, nor things to come, Nor height, nor depth, nor any other creature, shall be able to separate us from the love of God, which is in Christ Jesus our Lord.*
>
> *(Romans 8:31-39- KJV)*

- *If I Perish, I Perish.* This is perhaps the hardest one for many times this is the reason why we back away and step out of our watchman position. We don't want to perish! It is often said that if you refuse to stand for something then you will fall for anything! Queen Esther learnt the truth of dying to oneself for the sake of the kingdom of God and ended up saving the lives of her people from what would have been sure slaughter (Esther 4:15-17). We see her as a hero but this is really the position that each believer and every watchman-intercessor should take. The more we hold on to our lives, we will lose it but if we choose to lose our lives for Christ's sake, it's a promise that we will find it (Matt. 10:39).

- *Find Others to Pray For in Similar Situations.* This is one of the surest ways that one can come out of a *'self-absorbed, feeling sorry for myself, nobody appreciates me, why am I even trying'* outlook. If as an intercessor your marriage is failing, apart from doing whatever you can to restore it, it is a good time to think of all the marriages that are struggling too and pray for them. If your child has been unruly, this is the time to pray for all the parents who are struggling with the same issue; and for their children who need a touch from God. This sounds contrary to the way we usually think and may even sound insensitive to some but becoming anxious and preoccupied with our own issues doesn't usually bring a godly solution. There is an interesting Scripture which could help us with this:

> *Therefore take unto you now seven bullocks and seven rams, and go to my servant Job, and offer up for yourselves a burnt offering; and my servant Job shall pray for you: for him will I accept: lest I deal with you after your folly, in that ye have not spoken of me the thing which is right, like my servant Job.*

*So Eliphaz the Temanite and Bildad the Shuhite and
Zophar the Naamathite went, and did according as the
LORD commanded them: the LORD also accepted Job.*

*And the LORD turned the captivity of Job, when he
prayed for his friends: also the LORD gave Job twice
as much as he had before.*

(Job 42:8-10 - KJV)

Job's healing and deliverance seems to be directly related to the fact that he prayed for his friends. Even though they had also said some hurtful things, God wanted Job's focus to be on praying for others. What a deliverance Job got – double for his trouble!

One of the hardest realities that a Christian and watchman-intercessor cannot afford to allow themselves to be deceived by embracing is that praying more, fasting more, walking in righteousness can exempt us from trials and suffering. In Psalm 23, David, who tells us about the Great Shepherd who restores his soul, also points out that he has to go through the "valley of the shadow of death" (Ps. 23:3-4). His close and nurturing relationship with the shepherd did not prevent him from going through dangerous spots on his journey. The realism of living on this side of heaven is that we all will see trouble of one kind or another (Job 5:7). The great news is that we go through the valley and are not left in it. The climax of this psalm and of the life of the believer in Christ is that goodness and mercy are our constant companions and bodyguards to keep us on the way and we will dwell in the house of the Lord forever (Ps 23:6)!

God is calling the watchmen-intercessors back into their positions on the wall where the gap has been left unattended. I am convinced that many doors have been flung open; many gates have been breached; many undesirable elements have snuck into our families, Churches and nations because the intercessors have been knocked down or have become distracted because of need. We cannot allow the fire of God to go out on God's altar of prayer. God is depending on us to arise, brush ourselves off and get going again with the business of the kingdom. If there is a strong reason for us to get back to form, apart from wanting to obey God, it is for posterity. The next generation needs to come into their purpose too. Our survival and success impacts heavily their own success. We cannot afford to fail God. We cannot afford to fail our children. We must leave for ourselves a legacy.

CHAPTER 13

Intercession in the Marketplaces

Because we've been entrenched in the "secular versus sacred" model for so long, it can be difficult for us to view our work as a ministry and workplace believers as missionaries in the 9 to 5 Window. However, God tells us clearly that we are to glorify God in all that we do.

-Os Hillman

ONE OF THE hardest things to do today is to start and sustain a business netting profits that keep you increasing your product or service and maintaining the work force to dispense with that product. In a study done in Jamaica in 2005, it was discovered that:

NEARLY HALF of Jamaican businesses fail to survive the early start-up years, a study conducted by the University of Technology (UTech) has found... Commissioned by the Global Entrepreneurship Monitor (GEM), the research project assesses entrepreneurial activity and provides information on entrepreneurship globally. Its 2005 report on Jamaica showed that of the approximately 391,000, or 17 per cent of Jamaicans who started or were planning on starting a new business, only 9.5 per cent of them survived within the first

*few years of being established. Of this 17 per cent, 241,500
were nascent entrepreneurs and 154,100 had established a
business within the 42 months prior to June 2005.*

(Nicholas Richards. "Jamaica failing its businesses".
Jamaica Gleaner, Friday, July 7, 2006)

Some questions one could ask are: Were Christians working in
these failed businesses? Were there persons praying for the prosperity
of the business? Were they taught that they should be praying for
their workplaces? Did some of these businesses belong to Christian
entrepreneurs? How was the body of Christ assisting in praying for the
survival and prosperity of these businesses? Hard questions I know but
it is working Christians and Christian businesses that bring tithes and
offerings into the Church; support missionaries and mission projects
locally and overseas and generally help to carry on the building of
the kingdom of God in tangible ways. Not to say that God cannot
or has not provided tithes through persons who are jobless but the
majority of the tithes and offerings come from the jobs which God has
provided for His people.

Sometimes believers do act as if their job is a separate affair from
their walk with God and they are the ones who go hunting for a
job – God has nothing to do with them getting the job. This is an
erroneous position since there are even instances, my own ministry
for example, where God created a job just in time for me to transition
into ministry and just when I needed it. In my case it was a ministry
job but there are several cases where this occurred for others outside
of an official full-time ministry setting. The Psalmist even tells us that
"For exaltation comes neither from the east nor from the west nor
from the south. But God is the Judge: He puts down one, and exalts
another." (Psa 75:6-7 - NKJV)

There must be an appreciation of this and this endorsement should also lead to a renunciation of a belief that many Christians have which is: business people are secular and we only pray for sacred things. Much of this comes from lack of knowledge and lack of training of and by church leaders.

> *Pastoral training generally happens in two contexts: in semi-naries and in churches. Here is where pastors-to-be learn how to pray and to lead people in prayer. Neither context, in my experience, emphasizes prayer for business...*

> *A high percentage of church members work in business. If churches are seeking to help people be disciples of Jesus in their daily lives, and most churches would say this is central to their mission, then it seems only natural for churches to address marketplace concerns, in teaching, preaching, and prayer.*

> *(www.beliefnet.com/columnists/markdroberts)*

Some Christians are also of the view that business people cannot be trusted. They are corrupt and especially if they are rich, they cannot be saved. Many of the movies that are watched portray business people as crooks, immoral, fraudulent and generally unethical. Although this might be true for some, being led astray by the love of money and the pursuit of selfish gain, this is not factual for all. There are genuine persons who have sought through the establishment of business, not only to legitimately feed their families, but to assist in community development, to sponsor charity organizations and to finance the furtherance of God's kingdom. The Church has often turned to businesses, even secular businesses, to assist in the sponsorship of their programmes. If this is the case, in what way does the Church support these businesses? The following are some specific reasons why businesses need intercessors.

Some Reasons to Intercede for Businesses

- *They meet our practical needs.* It is businesses that are responsible for meeting our everyday physical needs as God does not pour food, clothing, shelter, etc. out of heaven.

- *There needs to be unity in the workplace.* Employer–employee relationships and those among the workers need to be civil for an atmosphere conducive to a high level of productivity. The principle laid out in Scriptures about the falling of any kingdom divided against itself, is true for the business places too (Matt. 12:25).

- *There are Christians in business.* There were people in the bible who were called of God who were also business people. For example, the apostle Paul who was one of the busiest men preaching the gospel was a tentmaker, even while serving in the Kingdom of God (Acts 18:3).

- *God loves business people.* God uses people in business in many ways to bless others. When Christians in business display a spirit of generosity it opens up many hearts to the gospel of Christ.

- *The failure of legitimate businesses affects the economy of a nation.* When businesses fail, it affects the national budget. There are fewer taxes to meet the general needs of the populace. Our hospitals, the poor, orphanages, roads, etc. become affected. We cannot afford to be indifferent to this important provision that God has given especially as we consider the ones who would be most vulnerable in the failure of an economy.

- *The pressure of maintaining a business can be a distraction for the Christian believer.* Until one enters the business world and faces the intense competition and demand on the entrepreneur's time to keep that business afloat, one might not understand the level of stress for the long-term sustenance of a business. Sometimes the spiritual commitment of the person in business is negatively affected. In some spheres, there is a cut-throat mentality that the business person is constantly faced with. The Christian in business cannot fight this in the flesh. There seems to be a more intense struggle to walk the narrow pathway to sustain one's integrity and not resort to underhanded methods, which many other businesses are engaged in, in order to survive. The entrepreneur therefore needs the backing of the Church, indeed intercessors, to assist in this fight.

- *There are businesses that God Himself has given.* There are business persons who God gave a vision about a business prospect. God laid out the blueprint and has engineered the way for prosperity. We may not know the inside story of many businesses but it is sufficient to know that God gave man a mind to do business. He should therefore get the glory from the way business is done and the end result of those businesses. Like anything else within the Church, this needs to be undergirded by prayer. There are Christians who for example were made redundant or lost their job for other reasons who cried out to God to provide another job. His question to them was: "What *is* that in your hand?" like He asked Moses (Exod. 4:2 - NKJV). This question was to draw their attention to the fact that the answer to their predicament was the very skills, talents and abilities which He had bestowed on them. That if they got busy using them in a structured way and with the end result to feed themselves and their families, He would prosper them. Would God highlight one's abilities to be made into a business and then turn His back, refusing to assist, when it was time to prosper that business?

Having said all of that, are there specific ways that the watchman-intercessor might be called to intercede within the Marketplace? Are there different prayers and a different modus operandi when it comes to praying in the public arena? One surprise discovery for me, was that a prayer ministry was actually set up to pray for the United Nations (UN). This ministry consisted of workers who carried a burden for the mission of the UN. The privilege was ours to be invited to the UN to be a part of that prayer initiative and to be addressed by ambassadors who shared with us the needs of the UN [http://webtv.un.org/watch/part-1-the-united-nations-prayer-initiative].

Another surprise was learning that there was a prayer ministry set up primarily for interceding in Hollywood –for the movie industry and those who work in it. The privilege was ours too to hear the passionate call for prayer for this industry which impacts on so many of our cultures and shapes so many of our homes and youth [hollywoodprayernetwork.org]. I must confess that I had never thought that praying for Hollywood would have been considered as a prayer initiative. This is why teaching is so necessary regarding prayer in the Marketplaces. It might never have occurred to a pastor that such prayers are indeed crucial and therefore it would not have been a pulpit or prayer room emphasis. Maybe our lack of knowledge has much to do with what the late Derek Prince had to say in his book *Secrets of a Prayer Warrior*:

Why do we Christians find it so hard to believe that so much depends on our praying? We take the attitude that what goes

*on is beyond our control. There is nothing we can do about it.
We complain, criticize. But we fail to pray. We have not understood the limitless possibilities of praying according to God's
will as revealed in His Word. Because of this, we fail to rule in
God's Kingdom the way He intends. (p 60)*

The fact is that we could and we should have people praying for
us to fulfill our purpose and calling in our workplaces and we should
be doing the same for others. This is taking the Kingdom of God
outside of the Church walls. This type of praying could happen within
a prayer room but sometimes it might be necessary to pray on-sight
where the watchmen-intercessors are able to discern even through
the natural senses what God wants to do in that place. Marketplace
intercession takes place where the masses are on a daily basis.

In an article done by Jericho Walls, "Establishing prayer groups
In churches and the marketplace", they suggested guidelines to
praying in the marketplaces.[www.globalprn.com/wp-content/
uploads/Establish-prayergroups-in-marketplace] Here are some of the
guidelines given:

Practical Guidelines

- Look for at least one other person to pray with, in your workplace or among your friends.

- Then ask others to join you in prayer, contacting them one by
  one.

- Start by praying together once a week. If you feel confident to
  add another prayer session

- after a couple of weeks, increase it to twice a week. Many prayer groups stagnate or stop because people attempt to meet for prayer on a daily basis. It seldom succeeds.

- If you have established a prayer group in the marketplace, ensure that the prayer meeting is held either before work or during a tea break or lunchtime. Only use time within business hours in exceptional cases and only if you have the clear go-ahead and support of management.

- If it is a prayer group in the marketplace, keep the time limit of the meetings to 30 minutes. Elsewhere an hour or hour and a half would do.

- Read a few relevant Scripture verses and make one or two short comments about that (do not spend more than 5 minutes on this). Allow time if someone wants to share what he/she learned about prayer. It is important to give time for 1-2 testimonies of answers on prayer.

- Give opportunity for people to share prayer requests at the start of the meeting, but be careful to avoid only praying for personal needs and physical healing during the time of prayer. Our responsibility to intercede is wider than that.

  a. Pray for issues at your work (decisions to be made, a crisis, contact with clients, etc.)

  b. Everyone praying for the salvation of 2-3 persons

  c. Pray for personal needs

  d. Pray for the government

e. Pray for at least one news headline topic, something having a significant impact on people in the country

f. Other issues you feel God laid on your hearts

Do not try to cover all these every time you pray. Three or four points are sufficient per meeting.

- There are various practical ways of praying. Make room for spontaneous prayer; divide the group into groups of 3-4 and pray for different issues. Everyone may pray simultaneously.

- Praise and worship is also a form of prayer. Do not, however, sing more than 2-3 songs per prayer meeting, as it may limit the time for prayer.

- Encourage people to pray Scripture.

Part of praying in the Marketplace is praying in the public square. This means that the intercessor might be called upon to pray at a public event, in a public arena. Prayers done in such a context are somewhat different from prayers prayed devotionally within the walls of a Church. One man of God who has trumpeted the cause of Marketplace praying is Bishop Dr. Peter Morgan, former senior pastor of the Covenant Community Church in Jamaica and currently President of the International Third World Leaders Association (ITWLA). He shares a few personal pointers on prayer in the Marketplace:

- The Marketplace is a valid context for blessing God's people. That was His first commitment when He said "Be fruitful, multiply, replenish the earth and subdue it."

- Jesus met people in the marketplace where their needs are

real and their relationships are open, more so than in the synagogues and Temple.

- Christians must see workplace as God's provision for their livelihood and for serving in and contributing to the well-being of their community.

- The people must see the Creator God as the source of their energy, productivity, creativity and purpose in the workplace.

- When praying, the language and style should be simple, straightforward, conversational and non-religious.

- Prayers should be as much for the proprietors/managers as for co-workers and for subordinates.

- Prayers must always be goal oriented and practical.

- Always remember that the people in the marketplace are more than "workers", they also have families, community concerns, etc.

- Leave them with the responsibility to care for each other.

Having been exposed to praying in the Marketplaces there are some principles that I have gleaned which could be beneficial to those who are already praying outside of the safety of Church walls or wish to extend their ministry to reach the unchurched. Here are some further guidelines for praying in the Marketplace:-

- The intercessor should be *modestly and appropriately dressed for the occasion.* In cultures where women wearing pants is offensive or they are expected to cover their heads, dressing accordingly would be appreciated by the masses. While in seminary, we were not permitted to wear pants to class or even within the library. Of course, many, though having to comply, felt that this was a ridiculous rule. Later however, having to minister in various churches where cultures differed and ministering in certain communities where Christians were expected to dress differently so they would not be mistaken for the people of the world, the necessity of this apparently unnecessary "edict" was realized. While in Israel, as women entering certain sites, our heads had to be covered. Those whose clothing was deemed not modest enough, had to wrap a scarf around themselves. Visiting the largest mosque in the United Arab Emirates (UAE), every female entering, whether Muslim or not, had to put on the garb that the Muslim women wear. The mosque supplies them. Paul spoke of becoming "… all things to all *men,* that I might by all means save some…" (1 Cor. 9:19-23 - NKJV). This is very applicable when ministering in the Marketplaces.

- *Protocol should be observed as far as is possible.* Praying in the Marketplace is a service before God. He is the One who gives us the privilege of praying in palaces and before Kings, Presidents, Prime Ministers and Managers. We should respect such a privilege by observing the status quo.

In Suriname where we hosted the second Caribbean Prayer Summit, when the President of Suriname arrived for the Opening Ceremony, I was summoned to meet him at the door. There was a particular order of the procession of which I was required to be a part. There was a particular seating order and only a few of us could be on the front row with the President. I was strongly led to pray for the President after he opened the Summit. This permission was asked of the local host-coordinator who in turn consulted with an assistant, who received the consent of the President. I was very aware while praying that I should not attempt to touch him. Why? There is a protocol about getting close to dignitaries and no matter how powerful we are as prayer warriors, this does not give us the right to cross certain boundary lines. If God requires a particular action, He usually prompts the official recipient who would ask, for example, for hands to be laid on him in prayer.

- *Wait for instructions especially when in an unfamiliar setting.* Although we are bold in our praying and not intimidated by persons, places or circumstances, we are still subject to persons who are in authority and should be respectful of their territory. We should wait to be led or given specific instructions. A table with a water jug and glasses might be laid out for specific persons and not for general use. Courtesy should be practiced by the watchman-intercessor in enquiring where it would be appropriate to acquire drinking water. This could also avoid any awkward and embarrassing encounters for the intercessor.

- *Observe limitations given.* When praying in the Marketplace, time restriction is usually more strongly observed than within the walls of the average Church. If the intercessor is given three minutes to pray then three minutes it is. God is not offended by a three-minute prayer and this can be done if he prepares himself adequately, spending time in the presence of the Lord beforehand so that he knows exactly where God wants him to focus his prayer.

- *Know whose authority you stand in.* Be prepared and therefore not display fear or an overwhelmed posture. It is natural for some persons when they are in the presence of dignitaries to feel somewhat clumsy concerning their performance. This often has very little to do with ability but with a sense of awe. This sense of amazement can cause the intercessor to foul up and lose focus on Who brought him there and whose power he needs to access to execute the prayer assignment. In other instances there might be apprehension. Every opportunity we receive to minister beyond the walls of the Church, we must see it as God who has opened a door and we are there in His authority, even in the face of a threat.

I was doing an annual seminar with some pastors and missionaries in a communist country. The team knew we were on assignment and was passionately fulfilling their mission. In the midst of my teaching and intercessory prayers and while the rest of the team were with the children, the authorities arrived. They commanded us, the visiting team, to stop what we were doing and to go immediately to the nearby police station. The local pastors and other leaders however insisted on coming with us. They were not going to let us face this alone. We had to go on the streets to find a truck to take all of us to the police station. When we arrived we were ushered inside where we all were questioned by four officials. Prayers were going up by us and on our behalf. We saw this as God giving us an opportunity to set the soles of our feet in such a significant place to pray.

While sitting there and listening to the interrogation being done in another language, the Holy Spirit spoke these words to me: *"They are in authority but so are you!"* Immediately

I had a sensing that God wanted to use me and I needed to stand in my authority. Boldness came upon me. I called on our translator to interpret every word I was about to say to the communist authorities without changing or toning anything. He agreed and I stood up to speak. I did so twice and at the end of the second address, the military official suddenly told us we were free to go. As we descended the stairs I wondered, "Did they recognize divine authority speaking through us?" We all left and went shopping.

We discovered later however that the senior local coordinator was told to report to a particular government ministry the following day. We knew that they were now targeting him. This could be trouble. We decided that he was not going alone. We were not going to abandon them in trouble. The weather changed overnight and there was a storm that developed in that region and was heading directly for the place where we were. With the threat of the storm, we headed for the ministry with the pastor and this turned out for us to be a prayer walk through that community. Upon arrival at the government building, it was locked - in preparation for the storm. As soon as we returned to the coordinator's home where the team was staying, the main road to that ministry building was blocked; barriers were placed in the middle of the road to block all forms of traffic. This was in preparation for the storm. There was no way for us to return the following days, neither would anyone be crossing over to where we were. The storm took centre stage. We stayed and rode out the storm with God's people. We were able to remain, continue fellowshipping and have great times of prayer for the nation and the people to be safe during the storm. We left by bus a couple days after, when we were due to leave, without harassment. Before this, sometimes upon leaving the police would come and demand our passports; interrogate us; search through our cameras, etc. Our team and the locals saw the power of God and had a life-impacting experience. We saw God answer prayers and shut down the operations within a nation to avert any disturbance to His will being carried out at that time.

- *Pray Identificational prayers standing in compassion and mercy.* It is always interesting to note how Jesus responded to persons he met in the Marketplaces. There was such tenderness in Him even while dealing with persons who obviously were in deep sin. His response to them however was with the heart of the Good Shepherd because He saw them as sheep without a shepherd (Matt. 9:36). He saw many who were like the people of Nineveh. They could not "discern between their right hand and their left hand." (Jonah 4:11- ASV). People like Daniel and Nehemiah who had to carry out the will of God within the Marketplace prayed and identified with the sins of the people, crying out to God for mercy (Nehemiah 1:6-7; Daniel 9:4-19). We are not in the Marketplace to point accusatory fingers at the prostitutes, criminals, etc. who might be standing there while we are praying but rather to allow the love of Jesus to flow from us to them, even while we pray for them.

- *Be prepared to humble yourself.* Some of the places we will be sent to minister in the Marketplaces will be way below our standard. You might be called to use sub-standard toilet facilities, which was the experience of a group of watchmen intercessors in West Africa. The toilet, when we arrived at one border, was a hole in the ground with two blocks around it to stand on and a piece of zinc to block the eyes of those passing on the main road. This experience was repeated in another Caribbean nation where intercessors were on assignment. This is not an attempt to create a crude picture or in any way to speak negatively of the circumstances of others but to present a reality that we will not always have our ideals met when we are sent by God into the Marketplace. Sometimes the intercessor might have to eat what is placed before him even when he cannot describe or discern what it is. Somehow God gives His people the grace to do what it takes to reach the masses who might never visit any Church.

On one intercessory-missionary trip, there was an intercessor from a developed country. She complained about being placed in a sub-standard bedroom in a pastor's home when she was accustomed, on previous missions trips, to stay in a hotel. We later discovered that the pastor and his children had given up their humble bedrooms and were sleeping in uncomfortable conditions packed in one room, in order to accommodate us. We were so humbled when we accidentally discovered the trouble this family went through for us to be comfortable while we ministered and interceded in that country.

- *Recognize that God fights for all the oppressed.* God is not just a God for Christians. He is interested in justice for all (Psalm 103:6). The intercessor therefore has to see his role in the Marketplace as one of bringing God's intervention into situations that trouble His heart. Situations of injustice and oppression; immorality and deception; corruption and abuse. Sometimes this might mean that God's watchmen-intercessors have to visit Parliament and pray as Government Ministers deliberate legislative affairs. They may have to sit through long hours of a trial in order to pray through for justice to be done.

They may have to visit the humble dwellings of the poor who are crying out for divine intervention when in trouble with no one to help them. *There are persons the watchman-intercessor will touch that others might not care to.*

- *Avoid the use of religious clichés that might not be understood by the unchurched.* There has been an interesting observation that has left me smiling many times. It is how we use clichés and abbreviations in our personal area(s) of discipline as if these are common terms that lay people know. This is done generally and it is true of us as Christians. We assume that everyone, especially unbelievers, understand the terms, "the Blood"; "the Enemy"; "born again"; "bind the Enemy", etc. I try to imagine being a non-Christian and how I might interpret "Enemy" (possibly as someone who did me something wrong, maybe a co-worker); "the blood" (what blood? Who does it belong to?) Get the gist?

Prayer should be seen as a vehicle through which we will be communicating with God on behalf of our listeners in the Marketplace and should be clearly expressed. They should understand what we are asking God for on their behalf and they should be able to agree with those petitions. Words are powerful but they lose their potency where there is lack of understanding. Have you ever listened to a speech and in response you were thinking, "Well, that was Greek to me!" Usually this response comes from someone who does not know the Greek language. In seminary we had to do two years of Greek. Believe me. At the beginning it was truly "Greek" to us new students until we got into the vocabulary, grammar and translation. It was feeling more like "English" to us (almost as clear as our first language).

- *Employ the critical discipline of fasting.* It is in the Marketplace that the watchman-intercessor could, like Jesus, encounter the most vicious demonic forces and attacks. Like Jesus said, "this kind goeth not out, but by prayer and fasting." (Matt. 17:21 - KJV). There are some tough situations and some stubborn seemingly unshakeable circumstances that will be faced while praying in the Marketplace but if the watchman-intercessor will employ the discipline of fasting and at least once per week, twin it with prayer, unbelievable breakthroughs result.

If watchmen-intercessors are deployed and even employed to do full-time intercession in the Marketplaces, many more businesses would prosper. If these intercessors were on hand to pray through difficult situations and to cover management and staff in prayer, I believe more Christian and even secular businesses would thrive. It is my hope that businesses would take up the challenge and intercessors will know when they are called to pray for and within business places to ensure the stability of these businesses and by extension, the economy of their nation.

The Church cannot exist well without its prayer-engine. The world cannot function well without prayer-backing and our individual and family lives will not see the great fulfillment of purpose unless we take up our positions in prayer. Watchmen-intercessors specifically called to this ministry have to rise up and fulfill their tasks so that the building and expansion of God's Kingdom can happen at the rate that God intends for it to occur.

A DECLARATION OVER ALL OF GOD'S WATCHMEN-INTERCESSORS

Those called from the womb will be born in their right season;

Those who are novices will grow up on a fast track and become fully equipped;

Those who are wounded and might have fallen by the wayside, will be instantly restored and transformed into the warriors that God has created them to be;

Those who might be in sin will be convicted, challenged and restored, walking in holiness and fulfilling their destiny.

Those who have been held back by curses and other weights will come into personal freedom and will pray others into liberty;

Those who have been serving faithfully will go several rungs up on the ladder of ministry, to the glory of God the Father.

Children-watchmen will be given a chance to grow and expand in the ministry of intercession, recognizing their call from their youth.

Intercessors will be connected in the spirit and in the natural with other intercessors receiving strength as they pray and share together.

Marketplace-intercessors will see the relevance of their presence and the impact of their prayers beyond the walls of the Church, impacting businesses and those on the highways and byways.

Prayer Warriors will win the battles they are fighting on the frontline for the Kingdom of God and will recover all that the Enemy has stolen from them and from the Body of Christ.

I DECLARE:

That *pastors and other Church leaders* along with *Intercessors* shall become a great team – a Dream Team

No longer will there be hurt and misunderstanding doing damage to the intercessory ministry and fellowships

Church leaders shall know too how to intercede and *intercessors will know* by divine illumination what it takes to shepherd a flock

Broken relationships between intercessors and their leaders will be mended and a strong team built to undergird the ministries within the churches. Nations shall be transformed because intercessors are healed and restored to their rightful positions in-the-gap on the walls.

Bibliography

Bright, B., & Cunningham, L. (1975). *The Seven Mountains of Influence in Culture. Retrieved from* www.7culturalmountains.org.

Earle, Ralph (Compiler). (1997). *Adam Clarke's Commentary on the Bible*. Nelson Reference; abridged edition.

Franklin, Jentezen. (2008). *Fasting: Opening the door to a deeper, more intimate, more powerful relationship with God*. USA: Charisma House: A Strang Company.

Hagin, Kenneth, E. (1992). *The Art of Prayer*. USA: Faith Library.

Ilnisky, Esther. (2012). *Let The Children Pray*. USA: Esther Network Intl./Children's Global Prayer Movement.

Payne, Dr. Karl I. (2011). *Spiritual Warfare*. WND Books.

Porter, Noah. Editor. (1913). *Webster's Revised Unabridged Dictionary*. G & C. Merriam Co.

Prince, Derek. (1990). *Blessing or Curse: You Can Choose*. USA: Chosen Books Pub Co.

Prince, Derek. (2009). *Secrets of a Prayer Warrior*. Grand Rapids : Baker Pub. Group.

Thomas Nelson Incorporated, World Bible Publishing. (1998) *God's Word: Today's Bible Translation that Says what it Means*. World Publishing Company

Vine, W. E., Unger, M.F., White, Jr., William. Editors. (1985). *Vine's Expository Dictionary of Biblical Words*. USA: Thomas Nelson Publishers.

Wagner, C. Peter. (1994). *Prayer Shield: How To Intercede for Pastors, Christian Leaders and Others On the Spiritual Frontlines*. Gospel Light, Revised Edition.

Pedrin, Michael. Clear Bible Answers. n.d. Retrieved from (http://clearbibleanswers.org)   http://www.jwipn.com/pdf/cywtp_chapter32

"Establishing Prayer Groups In Churches And The Marketplace" n.d, Retrieved from [www.globalprn.com/wp-content/uploads/Establish-prayergroups-in-marketplace]

KJV Dictionary (av1611.com/kjbp/kjv-dictionary/groan.html)(www.royalkids.org)

Otis Jr., George. Director. *'Transformations II'* Video/DVD Series. Global Net Productions.

Senyonga, Jackson, n.d *"Revival the Hard Way"*. Retrieved fromChristianity Today International. [www.Christianity.com]

Kenneth E. Hagin. n.d. Kenneth Hagin Ministries: (www.rhema.org).

Teresa Seputis. *"A Spiritual Checkup For Intercessors"*. Retrieved from [http://www.godspeak.net]

Matt Holcomb, Submission to Spiritual Authority. Retrieved from http://bromatt.wordpress.com/2009/06/22/submission-to-spiritual-authority

"Bitterness: The Subtle Killer." Retrieved from [http://powered-by-adversity.com/adversity/barriers/bitterness.php]

Richards, Nicholas. (Friday, July 7, 2006). *"Jamaica failing its businesses"*. Jamaica *Gleaner*Roberts, Mark D. *Praying For Business*. Retrieved from [www.beliefnet.com/columnists/markdroberts]

Jericho Wall. *"Establishing prayer groups In churches and the marketplace"*. Retrieved from [www.globalprn.com/wp-content/uploads/Establish-prayergroups-in-marketplace]

About the Author

MARIA HARBAJAN IS President and CEO of the National Intercessory Prayer Network of Jamaica / Prayer Centre of the Caribbean (NIPNOJ/ P-COC). She is an ordained minister and has been involved in the ministry of intercession for over 30 years. She is host of a radio pro-gramme, *"ARISE AND BUILD JAMAICA"*, calling the nation to rise up in prayer and action to build the Kingdom of God. This is aired on LOVE FM in Jamaica.

Mrs. Harbajan has known Jesus as her personal Saviour since she was 15 years old. She obtained a Bachelor's degree in Theology from the Jamaica Theological Seminary and a Master's degree in Counselling Psychology at the Caribbean Graduate School of Theology. She also holds a Doctorate in Ministry, from Central Christian University and did Leadership studies at the Haggai Institute in Singapore in 2000.

Mrs. Harbajan entered full-time ministry for two years ('85 - '87), paused to study and resumed in 1991.

She is a member of the Executive Team of the International Prayer Council as convener of the Caribbean Prayer Summit which has been held in Barbados, Suriname and Jamaica. Founder and senior counsellor of the OASIS Counselling Services and founder of the OASIS Restoration Ministries International, a ministry that seeks to restore individuals, families, businesses, etc. to their purpose in God. A speaker at conferences, camps, schools, churches, etc. She covers a variety of topics including Family and Marital Relationships, Intercession, Spiritual Warfare, Stress Management, Issues Involving Young People, and personal issues that affect people in the workplace. She has ministered internationally in the Middle East, Africa, Asia, Europe, the Caribbean, Central and South America.

Mrs. Harbajan is involved in Missions, teaching pastors and other leaders on the Mission field. A leader at the Portmore Gospel Assembly, St. Catherine, Jamaica, she is married to Devon Harbajan, a Minister of Religion and they have a son DeMario Samuel.

FOR FURTHER INFORMATION:

MARIA HARBAJAN, DMin, M.A., B.Th.

President and CEO, National Intercessory Prayer Network of Jamaica
Founder/Senior Counsellor, OASIS Counselling Services
Founder, OASIS Restoration Ministries International
Regional Coordinator, Caribbean Prayer Summit
Member of the Executive, International Prayer Council

Call 876-806-4921 or 876-967-4041 (office)

E-mail address:
mardevharb@cwjamaica.com / prayernet@cwjamaica.com.

CPSIA information can be obtained
at www.ICGtesting.com
Printed in the USA
BVHW01s1745080218
507489BV00002B/177/P